TALMUD
FOR EVERYDAY LIVING

EMPLOYER-EMPLOYEE RELATIONS

HILLEL GAMORAN

UAHC Press
New York, NY

Typesetting: El Ot Ltd.
This book is printed on acid-free paper.
Copyright © 2001 by Hillel Gamoran
Manufactured in the United States of America

10 9 8 7 6 5 4 3 2 1

Dedication

From as early as I can remember until I graduated from high school, I had a Hebrew lesson every evening after dinner. When I was small, my teacher was my mother; my father taught my older brother. When my younger sister became old enough for lessons, then my mother taught her and my father taught my brother and me together. During my last three years of high school, when my brother was a college student, my father taught just me.

We began with simple stories and later advanced to Bible, Talmud and modern Hebrew literature.

It was, without a doubt, as a result of those Hebrew lessons that I developed an appreciation and a love for the Hebrew language, the Bible and the Talmud.

This book is lovingly dedicated to the memory of my mother, Mamie G. Gamoran and my father, Emanuel Gamoran, who first taught me Torah.

Acknowledgements

Many thanks to the members of Beth Tikvah Congregation, Hoffman Estates, Illinois, who attended adult education classes over the years when the passages from the Talmud which appear in this book were the subject of study and discussion. Their questions, comments and insights have enriched the pages of this work.

Thanks are also due to the members of Temple Beth Am, Seattle, Washington, for engaging an earlier version of this material and for offering many valuable suggestions.

I wish to express my debt to my editor, Rabbi Hara Person, whose wisdom, skill and good humor made it possible to translate an idea into a finished product. I would also like to thank Debra Hirsch Corman, Liane Broido, Stuart Benick and Ken Gesser for their help.

The greatest gift one can find is a partner with whom to share one's life with love and loyalty. I have been so blessed. My thanks to my wife, Judith, for her support, encouragement and editorial input all along the way.

Contents

Introduction   ix

Brief Definitions   xiii

Guide to Text Type   xiii

Talmudic Sages   xiv

CHAPTER ONE
The Employment Contract   1

CHAPTER TWO
Quitting Before a Job Is Completed   13

CHAPTER THREE
How Long Is the Workday?   18

CHAPTER FOUR
Eating at the Employer's Expense   23

CHAPTER FIVE
Prompt Payment   37

CHAPTER SIX
Conflicting Claims   49

CHAPTER SEVEN
Wrapping It Up   58

Sources for Further Study   63

Introduction

The Talmud is the most informative of the classic works of Judaism. The rules for praying, for eating, for marrying and divorcing, for observing the Sabbath and the Festivals, for buying and selling, for borrowing and lending, for almost every aspect of living, are covered in the Talmud. Someone who wants to know the source of the beliefs and practices of Judaism should turn to the Talmud.

What is the Talmud, and how did it come to be?

In the centuries following the completion of the Torah, when Jews had questions about the meaning of the biblical laws, they turned to judges and scholars for answers. Few of the responses from the Second Temple period (about 516 B.C.E. to 70 C.E.) have been preserved, nor are the names of most of the Sages of this period known. But the names of Hillel and Shammai, who lived in the first century B.C.E. and were the foremost scholars of their time, have been retained. Two academies that bore their names flourished during the first century C.E., and a large number of the teachings of those academies have been preserved.

Though many legal decisions were made and interpretations of the Torah offered over the course of the centuries, no attempt was made to formulate a comprehensive law for the Jewish people until after the destruction of the Second Temple in 70 C.E. After that national catastrophe, enormous changes took place. The place that had been the center of Jewish life for the preceding 600 years was no longer. The chief Jewish ritual, animal sacrifice, ceased to exist. The priests lost their primary function. The military, the government, and the aristocracy had all been crushed. In fact, many believed that Judaism had come to an end.

At that time, when hope for Jewish continuity was waning, a group of Sages, led by Rabbi Yochanan ben Zakkai, gathered in the coastal town of Yavneh and began the process of creating a law for the Jewish people that could exist independently of the Temple. It was during this period that synagogues, which had existed for hundreds of years, began to be seen as a replacement for the Temple, that prayer was deemed an acceptable substitute for sacrifice and that rabbis, rather than priests, were acknowledged as the leaders of the Jewish community.

The law was further developed during the second century C.E., when the leading figure was Rabbi Akiva ben Joseph. He is credited with organizing the law according to topics and subtopics. His arrangement of the law and his interpretations of previous rulings became dominant, and his students became the leading Sages of the next generation, establishing academies throughout Palestine.

About 200 C.E. the central rabbinic academy was headed by Rabbi Judah HaNasi (Judah the Patriarch). Rabbi Judah and his associates relied on the teachings of Rabbi Akiva's students to create a work called the Mishnah. The Mishnah was a compilation of laws, composed in lucid Hebrew, divided into six orders, each order into tractates, each tractate into chapters, and each chapter into paragraphs. The six orders of the Mishnah deal with the following:

1. Agricultural law
2. Holiday law
3. Family law
4. Civil and criminal law
5. Temple law
6. Purity law

From the time of its publication, the Mishnah became the foundation of Jewish law. It was studied in the academies of Palestine and Babylonia; its principles were analyzed, contradictions were resolved, and it was used as the basis for legal decisions. The discussions of the Mishnah in the academies were compiled and edited in Palestine about 400 C.E. and in Babylonia about 500 C.E. These discussions are called the Gemara. The Mishnah and the Gemara together constitute the Talmud.

The Jerusalem Talmud shows signs of often being incomplete and disjointed; it was not widely studied after its completion. The Babylonian Talmud, on the other hand, was carefully crafted and highly edited. Though its editors did not have transcriptions of the academy discussions, they had a voluminous tradition of questions, answers, and debates on the issues of law covered in the Mishnah. With the traditions before them and with boldness, skill, and creativity, the editors of the Babylonian Talmud succeeded in their task far beyond their expectations. For 1,500 years, the Babylonian Talmud has been the central focus of Jewish learning.

The discussions of the law in the Babylonian Talmud are often long and protracted. The arguments go back and forth over pages of text. At times, even after a sustained debate, the Talmud does not draw a conclusion as to what the correct ruling is. It would not be wrong to say that the editors of the Talmud were more interested in the logic of the arguments than in determining what the law should be. More than a passion for the law, they had a passion for the study of the law.

Many Jews today govern their lives by religious practices founded on talmudic law. Sabbath and holiday observances, regulations covering marriage and divorce, prayers and rituals, dietary restrictions, and more are all based on laws rooted in the Talmud. And even Jews who do not feel bound by laws based on the Talmud are still strongly influenced by its teachings in their beliefs and practices.

The material in this book deals with only one small aspect of talmudic law. It comes from the second tractate (called *Bava Metzia,* meaning "the middle gate") of the fourth order (called *N'zikin,* meaning "damages") of the Babylonian Talmud. The selections on employer-employee relationships have been chosen because they shed light on the life of our people some 1,500 years ago, because they illustrate the style of talmudic logic and reasoning, and because, we believe, the reader will find that many of the issues of law and equity that arose in ancient times are still relevant today.

Brief Definitions

Mishnah: The code of Jewish law compiled under the leadership of Rabbi Judah HaNasi about 200 C.E.

Gemara: The discussion of the law in the academies after the completion of the Mishnah.

Talmud: The Mishnah and the Gemara together.

baraita: A statement in the Gemara coming from the time of the Mishnah, but not included in the Mishnah.

Tanna: A rabbinic Sage from the period of the Mishnah, that is, before 200 C.E.

Amora: A rabbinic Sage of the Gemara, that is, one who lived between 200 and 500 C.E.

Guide to Text Type

The text of the Talmud in this book is printed in **bold type.**

The editor's comments are in regular type.

THE MISHNAH IS PRINTED IN CAPITAL LETTERS.

THE *BARAITOT* ARE PRINTED IN SMALL CAPITAL LETTERS.

The Gemara is printed in lowercase letters.

TANNAIM

Year C.E. (approx.)	Generation	
90	1	R. Yochanan b. Zakkai
130	2	R. Joshua, R. Akiva, R. Tarfon, R. Eleazar Chisma
160	3	R. Meir, R. Simeon, R. Judah, R. Jose, R. Simeon b. Gamaliel, R. Yochanan b. Matya
200	4	R. Judah HaNasi, R. Dosa, Issi b. Judah
220	5	R. Chiyya

AMORAIM

Year C.E. (approx.)	Generation	Palestine	Babylonia
250	1	R. Yannai	Rav, Samuel, R. Assi
290	2	R. Yochanan, Resh Lakish	R. Huna
320	3	R. Eleazar, R. Abahu	Rabbah, R. Chisda, R. Joseph, R. Acha b. R. Joseph
350	4		Abaye, Rava
375	5		R. Pappa, R. Shesha b. R. Idi
425	6		R. Ashi, R. Kahana, Maremar, Mar Zutra

Chapter One

The Employment Contract

הַשּׂוֹכֵר אֶת הָאוּמָּנִין וְהִטְעוּ זֶה אֶת זֶה, אֵין לָהֶם זֶה עַל זֶה אֶלָּא תַּרְעוֹמֶת.

Mishnah: **IF SOMEONE HIRED ARTISANS AND ONE MISLED THE OTHER, THE ONE WHO WAS MISLED HAS GROUNDS ONLY FOR RESENTMENT AGAINST THE OTHER.**

הַאי תַּנָּא "חָזְרוּ" נַמִי "הִטְעוּ" קָרֵי לֵיהּ. דְּתַנְיָא: הַשּׂוֹכֵר אֶת הָאוּמָּנִין וְהִטְעוּ אֶת בַּעַל הַבַּיִת, אוֹ בַּעַל הַבַּיִת הִטְעָה אוֹתָן, אֵין לָהֶם זֶה עַל זֶה אֶלָּא תַּרְעוֹמֶת. בַּמֶּה דְּבָרִים אֲמוּרִים? שֶׁלֹּא הָלְכוּ.

אֲבָל הָלְכוּ חַמָּרִים וְלֹא מָצְאוּ תְּבוּאָה, פּוֹעֲלִין וּמָצְאוּ שָׂדֶה כְּשֶׁהִיא לַחָה, נוֹתֵן לָהֶן שְׂכָרָן מִשְׁלֵם, אֲבָל אֵינוֹ דוֹמֶה הַבָּא טָעוּן לַבָּא רֵיקָן, עוֹשֶׂה מְלָאכָה לְיוֹשֵׁב וּבָטֵל.

The Mishnah's statement means that the one who was misled has grounds for resentment but has no grounds for a court case. However, the Mishnah does not explain how the worker or the employer was misled.

1

The Gemara seeks to answer this question by stating that: **When the author of the Mishnah said "misled," he meant "retracted,"** meaning that if an artisan who was hired to do a job backed out of his agreement, the employer could not sue the artisan in court; he had grounds only for resentment. By the same token, if the employer broke the contract, the artisan could not collect in court for damages; he could only be resentful of the employer's actions.

The Gemara questions whether this ruling applies under all circumstances: **For we have learned in a *baraita:* If someone hired artisans and they misled the employer, or the employer misled them, the one who was misled has grounds only for resentment against the other. Under what circumstances does this ruling apply? When they did not go to the place of work.**

What's Your Opinion?

Is this a fair ruling? If the worker was informed before leaving for work that his job was canceled, is it right that the employer who broke the contract not be required to pay compensation? Do you think that the question about an employer's liability for breaking a contract should depend not on whether or not the worker came to the job, but rather on whether or not the worker gave up other opportunities for work in order to do this job?

Consider This Case

Reuben hired Simon to paint his house. One week before the starting date, Reuben's car broke down, and he had to buy a new car. Under the circumstances, he felt that he couldn't afford to have his house painted, so he canceled his contract with Simon. Should Reuben have to pay Simon? Suppose the reason that Reuben canceled the contract was because someone else offered to do the job for less money. Would that make a difference in your answer?

The Gemara's citation of the *baraita* continues: **BUT IF ASS DRIVERS WENT AND DID NOT FIND PRODUCE TO HAUL, OR IF WORKERS WENT AND FOUND THAT THE FIELD WAS WATERLOGGED, THEN THE EMPLOYER MUST GIVE THEM THEIR WAGES IN FULL. BUT SOMEONE WHO CARRIES A LOAD IS NOT LIKE SOMEONE WHO TRAVELS EMPTY-HANDED, AND SOMEONE WHO WORKS IS NOT LIKE SOMEONE WHO SITS AND IS IDLE.**

How much should someone be paid who comes to work and finds that there is no work to do, because, for example, the field is waterlogged? At first the *baraita* says that he should be paid "in full," but then it suggests that payment in full may not be necessary, for, after all, "someone who carries a load is not like someone who travels empty-handed, and someone who works is not like someone who sits and is idle." The *baraita* thus rules that although a worker who comes and finds nothing to do must be paid, he does not have to be paid at the same rate as someone who actually performs a job. Since he sits and is idle, a lesser payment is adequate.

Bava Metzia 76b-77a

תָּנֵי תַּנָּא קַמֵּיה דְּרַב: נוֹתֵן לָהֶם שְׂכָרָן מְשָׁלֵם. אָמַר לֵיה: חֲבִיבִי אָמַר: אִילּוּ אֲנָא הֲוַאי, לָא הֲוָה יָהֵיבְנָא לָהֶן אֶלָּא כְּפוֹעֵל בָּטֵל, וְאַתְּ אָמְרַתְּ נוֹתֵן לָהֶם שְׂכָרָן מְשָׁלֵם. וְהָא עֲלָה קָתָנֵי: אֵינוֹ דוֹמֶה הַבָּא טָעוּן לְהַבָּא רֵיקָן, עוֹשֶׂה מְלָאכָה לְיוֹשֵׁב וּבָטֵל.

לָא סַיַּימוּהָ קַמֵּיה.

אִיכָּא דְּאָמְרִי: סַיַּימוּהָ קַמֵּיה, וְהָכִי קָאָמַר: חֲבִיבִי אָמַר: אִי הֲוַאי אֲנָא לָא הֲוָה יָהֵיבְנָא לֵיה כְּלָל, וְאַתְּ אָמְרַתְּ כְּפוֹעֵל בָּטֵל.

אֶלָּא קַשְׁיָא הָךְ.

לָא קַשְׁיָא. הָא דְּסַיְּירָא לְאַרְעֵיה מֵדְּאוֹרְתָּא, הָא דְּלָא סַיְּירָא לְאַרְעֵיה מֵאוֹרְתָּא.

3

כִּי הָא דַּאֲמַר רָבָא: הַאי מַאן דַּאֲגַר אֲגִירֵי לְרַפְקָא, וְאָתָא מִטְרָא וּמַלְיֵיה מַיָּא. אִי סַיְּירָא לְאַרְעֵיה מֵאוּרְתָּא פְּסֵידָא דְפוֹעֲלִים, לָא סַיְּירָא לְאַרְעֵיה מֵאוּרְתָּא, פְּסֵידָא דְּבַעַל הַבַּיִת, וְיָהֵיב לְהוּ כְּפוֹעֵל בָּטֵל.

וַאֲמַר רָבָא: הַאי מַאן דְּאוֹגִיר אֲגוֹרֵי לְדַוְולָא, וְאָתָא מִטְרָא, פְּסֵידָא דְפוֹעֲלִים. אָתָא נַהֲרָא, פְּסֵידָא דְּבַעַל הַבַּיִת, וְיָהֵיב לְהוּ כְּפוֹעֵל בָּטֵל.

וַאֲמַר רָבָא: הַאי מַאן דְּאוֹגִיר אֲגוֹרֵי לְדַוְולָא, וּפְסַק נַהֲרָא בְּפַלְגָא דְיוֹמָא. אִי לָא עֲבִיד דְּפָסֵיק, פְּסֵידָא דְפוֹעֲלִים. עֲבִיד דְּפָסֵיק, אִי בְּנֵי מָתָא, פְּסֵידָא דְפוֹעֲלִים, לָאו בְּנֵי מָתָא, פְּסֵידָא דְּבַעַל הַבַּיִת.

וַאֲמַר רָבָא: הַאי מַאן דַּאֲגַר אֲגוֹרֵי לַעֲבִידְתָּא וּשְׁלִים עֲבִידְתָּא בְּפַלְגָא דְיוֹמָא, אִי אִית לֵיה עֲבִידְתָּא דְּנִיחָא מִינָּה, יָהֵיב לְהוּ, אִי נַמִי, דַּכְוָתָה, מַפְקַד לְהוּ, דִּקְשָׁה מִינָּה, לָא מַפְקַד לְהוּ, וְנוֹתֵן לָהֶם שְׂכָרָן מְשָׁלֵם. אַמַּאי? וְלֵיתֵיב לְהוּ כְּפוֹעֵל בָּטֵל.

כִּי קָאָמַר רָבָא בְּאַכְלוּשֵׁי דִּמָחוֹזָא, דְּאִי לָא עָבְדִי חָלְשֵׁי.

The Gemara continues: **It was taught in Rav's presence, HE MUST GIVE THEM THEIR WAGES IN FULL. Rav said, "My uncle, Rav Chiyya, said, 'Had I been there, I would have paid them only as idle workers, and not, as the *baraita* says, "IN FULL."'"**

The Gemara expresses surprise at this statement attributed to Rav Chiyya:

Surely the *baraita* taught: SOMEONE WHO CARRIES A LOAD IS NOT LIKE SOMEONE WHO TRAVELS EMPTY-HANDED, AND SOMEONE WHO WORKS IS NOT LIKE SOMEONE WHO SITS AND IS IDLE. Since this teaching clearly modified the previous statement requiring payment in full, why did Rav Chiyya think that the *baraita* required a full payment?

The Gemara answers: **Rav Chiyya did not hear the concluding portion of the *baraita*.**

The reason that Rav Chiyya raised his objection was that he only heard that part of the *baraita* requiring payment in full but, for some reason, did not hear the statement that one who is idle need not receive full wages.

The Gemara then offers another version of Rav Chiyya's statement: **There are others who say that Rav Chiyya did hear the concluding portion of the *baraita* and that this is what Rav said: My uncle said: If I had been there, I would not have paid him anything at all, but you say that he should be paid as an idle worker.**

But the Gemara finds a difficulty with this version of Rav Chiyya's statement: **This is a contradiction.** How could Rav Chiyya have said that workers who come to a place of work and find that there is no work to do not be paid anything at all if a *baraita* says that they should be paid? How could Rav Chiyya contradict the ruling of a *baraita*? A *baraita* is an authoritative tannaitic statement, and an *Amora* (or a Sage like Rav Chiyya, who lived at the end of the tannaitic period) could never dispute a tannaitic ruling.

The Gemara responds: **There is no contradiction. Rav Chiyya's opinion, that the worker should not be paid, refers to a case where the employer checked his land the previous evening to see that it was workable. The statement in the *baraita* refers to a case where the employer did not check his land the previous evening.**

Many pages of the Gemara are devoted to pointing out contradictions within the tannaitic sources and to resolving these contradictions. The contradictions were within a Mishnah, between two different *mishnayot*, between a Mishnah and a *baraita,* or between two *baraitot*. The contradiction raised here is between a *baraita* and a statement of Rav Chiyya. Since Rav Chiyya lived at the end of the tannaitic period and is considered a semi-*Tanna*, his words almost have the authority of a *baraita*. Contradictions are usually resolved by applying one statement to one set of circumstances and the other statement to another set of circumstances. This is indeed how the contradiction raised here is resolved.

What's Your Opinion?

Does this seem reasonable? Is it right that the worker should get no payment at all if, when the landowner checked his property the previous evening, it was ready to be worked but, by the next day, it was unworkable? Is it right that the worker should receive compensation for coming to the job if the landowner neglected to check his property the previous evening?

Rava was the foremost Sage of the Babylonian Talmud. He lived in the middle of the fourth century and founded an academy at Mechoza on the Tigris River. His name appears in the Talmud more often than any other teacher, and his decisions are normally cited as authoritative. His debates with Abaye, as recorded in the Gemara, represent the high point of talmudic reasoning and rhetoric. Many rulings of Rava are cited by the Sages of later generations.

The Gemara continues by pointing out that Rava made a ruling in such a case: **Just as Rava said: If someone hired workers for digging, and it rained and filled the field with water, if he checked his land the previous evening, the loss is the workers'. If he did not check his field the previous evening, the loss is the employer's, and he must pay them as idle workers.**

The Gemara continues by giving three more rulings of Rava that are similar in nature: **This is just as Rava said: If someone hired workers for irrigation, and it rained, the loss is the workers'. If the river overflowed, the loss is the employer's, and he must give them their wages as idle workers.**

Rava assumes that rain is unpredictable, whereas the employer is expected to know if a river is likely to overflow.

And Rava said: If someone hired workers for irrigation, and the river from which the workers took the water stopped flowing in the middle of the day, if it doesn't often stop flowing, the loss is the workers'. If it frequently stops flowing, if the workers are from that locality, the loss is the workers'. If they are not from that locality, the loss is the employer's.

And Rava said: If someone hired people to do work, and the work was finished in the middle of the day, if the employer has other work to assign them that is easier than the work for which they were hired, he may give it to them. If it is

equal to the work for which they were hired, he may give it to them. If it is harder than the work for which they were hired, he may not assign it to them and must pay them their wages in full.

The Gemara expresses surprise that Rava requires that the workers be paid in full for the balance of the day: **Why should they be paid in full? Let him pay them as idle workers.**

When Rava said this, he was referring to the porters of Mechoza, who become weak if they do not work.

From Rava's rulings we learn of numerous happenings that prevented laborers from doing their jobs: (1) Rain waterlogged the fields. (2) Rain made irrigation unnecessary. (3) Rivers overflowed. (4) Rivers stopped flowing. (5) Work was completed sooner than expected. Rava's rulings explained when an employer was required to pay a laborer who had come to his job but was prevented from working and when he was exempt from paying the worker.

What's Your Opinion?

Do you agree with Rava's rulings regarding when a worker who was prevented from doing his job had to be paid?

Do you accept the Gemara's explanation as to why Rava stated that workers had to be paid in full for the second half of the day? Why else might one think that they should be paid?

Consider This Case

Ace Heating & Ventilation Contractors installed 10 percent of a $200,000 air-conditioning system in the Park View Apartments when several of the apartments became vacant and Park View had difficulty finding new tenants. The owners of the apartments decided that it would be prudent not to go ahead with plans for the air-conditioning. Ace demanded payment in full, according to the contract, whether or not the work was done. Park View offered $10,000 in addition to the $20,000 that had already been paid. What would be a just solution to this problem?

שָׂכַר אֶת הַחַמָּר וְאֶת הַקַּדָּר לְהָבִיא פְּרָיְיפָרִין וַחֲלִילִים לַכַּלָּה אוֹ לַמֵּת, וּפוֹעֲלִין לְהַעֲלוֹת פִּשְׁתָּנוֹ מִן הַמִּשְׁרָה, וְכָל דָּבָר שֶׁאָבֵד, וְחָזְרוּ בָּהֶן, מָקוֹם שֶׁאֵין שָׁם אָדָם, שׂוֹכֵר עֲלֵיהֶן אוֹ מַטְעָן.

The Mishnah now considers a situation in which breaking a contract would cause irreparable damage: **IF SOMEONE HIRED AN ASS DRIVER OR A WAGON DRIVER TO BRING POLES OR FLUTES FOR A WEDDING OR A FUNERAL, OR IF SOMEONE HIRED WORKERS TO BRING HIS FLAX OUT OF THE STEEPING POND, OR FOR ANY JOB WHERE THE EMPLOYER WOULD SUFFER A LOSS IF THE CONTRACT WERE BROKEN, THEN IF THE WORKERS RETRACT AND THERE ARE NO OTHER WORKERS AVAILABLE TO DO THE JOB, HE MAY HIRE OTHER WORKERS AT THEIR EXPENSE OR HE MAY DECEIVE THEM.**

בְּדָבָר הָאָבוּד, שׂוֹכֵר עֲלֵיהֶן אוֹ מַטְעָן. כֵּיצַד מַטְעָן? אוֹמֵר לָהֶן: סֶלַע קָצַצְתִּי לָכֶם, בֹּאוּ וּטְלוּ שְׁתַּיִם.

וְעַד כַּמָּה שׂוֹכֵר עֲלֵיהֶן? עַד אַרְבָּעִים וַחֲמִשִּׁים זוּז. בַּמֶּה דְּבָרִים אֲמוּרִים? בִּזְמַן שֶׁאֵין שָׁם פּוֹעֲלִים לִשְׂכּוֹר, אֲבָל יֵשׁ שָׁם פּוֹעֲלִים לִשְׂכּוֹר, וְאָמַר צֵא וּשְׂכוֹר מֵאֵלּוּ, אֵין לוֹ עֲלֵיהֶן אֶלָּא תַּרְעוֹמֶת.

The Gemara includes a passage from the same *baraita* cited above, which elaborates on the Mishnah: **IN THE CASE OF WHERE AN EMPLOYER WILL SUFFER A LOSS IF WORKERS BREAK A CONTRACT, HE MAY HIRE OTHER WORKERS AT THEIR EXPENSE OR HE MAY DECEIVE THEM. HOW MAY HE DECEIVE THEM? HE MAY SAY TO THEM: I PROMISED TO PAY YOU A *SELA*. COME AND TAKE TWO.**

AND HOW HIGH MAY HE GO TO HIRE REPLACEMENT WORKERS AT THEIR EXPENSE? UP TO FORTY OR FIFTY *ZUZ*.

A *sela*, in talmudic times, was a frequently used silver coin. A *zuz*, also called a *dinar*, was a smaller silver coin, one-fourth the value of a *sela*.

UNDER WHAT CIRCUMSTANCES DOES THIS APPLY? WHEN THERE ARE NO OTHER WORKERS AVAILABLE THERE TO HIRE AND HE HAS TO HIRE FROM ANOTHER LOCALITY. BUT IF THERE ARE OTHER WORKERS AVAILABLE IN THAT LOCALITY, AND THE WORKERS WHO RETRACTED SAID TO HIM, "GO AND HIRE FROM AMONG THEM," THEN HE MUST HIRE FROM AMONG THEM, AND HE HAS GROUNDS ONLY FOR RESENTMENT.

What's Your Opinion?

If a job has to be done at a certain time and a worker backs out of his agreement to do it, is it right for the employer to deceive the worker by promising him a payment that will not be made?

If a worker breaks a contract to perform a job that cannot be delayed, is it right that the employer may spend whatever is necessary to get the job done and may charge it to the one who reneged on his contract?

If a worker breaks a contract and other workers are available to do the job for the same pay, is it right that even though the employer might be resentful that he has to go to the trouble of hiring new workers, he does not receive any compensation for his trouble?

Consider This Case

Imagine the following situation: Johnny Bench, the all-star catcher for the Cincinnati Reds, has a long-term contract with his ball club but is unhappy because he is being paid far below what other players of similar or lesser skill are receiving.

Three days before the World Series, Bench demands a $1 million bonus to play in the Series. If he doesn't get his bonus, he vows not to play.

The owners of the Reds meet with Bench and sign a contract agreeing to pay Bench the additional million.

Now the Series is over. Bench's heroics have helped the Reds to win the Series, but the Reds' owners refuse to give Bench the promised bonus, arguing that the new contract was forced upon them and that they will not submit to blackmail.

Do you believe that the court should require the Reds to give Bench his bonus?

Bava Metzia 75b

Mishnah: **IF SOMEONE HIRED ARTISANS AND ONE MISLED THE OTHER, THE ONE WHO WAS MISLED HAS GROUNDS ONLY FOR RESENTMENT AGAINST THE OTHER.**

Bava Metzia 76b

Gemara: **When the author of the Mishnah said "misled," he meant "retracted."**

For we have learned in a *baraita:* IF SOMEONE HIRED ARTISANS AND THEY MISLED THE EMPLOYER, OR THE EMPLOYER MISLED THEM, THE ONE WHO WAS MISLED HAS GROUNDS ONLY FOR RESENTMENT AGAINST THE OTHER. UNDER WHAT CIRCUMSTANCES DOES THIS RULING APPLY? WHEN THEY DID NOT GO TO THE PLACE OF WORK.
BUT IF ASS DRIVERS WENT AND DID NOT FIND PRODUCE TO HAUL, OR IF WORKERS WENT AND FOUND THAT THE FIELD WAS WATERLOGGED, THEN THE EMPLOYER MUST GIVE THEM THEIR WAGES IN FULL. BUT SOMEONE WHO CARRIES A LOAD IS NOT LIKE SOMEONE WHO TRAVELS EMPTY-HANDED, AND SOMEONE WHO WORKS IS NOT LIKE SOMEONE WHO SITS AND IS IDLE.

Bava Metzia 76b-77a

It was taught in Rav's presence, HE MUST GIVE THEM THEIR WAGES IN FULL. Rav said, "My uncle, Rav Chiyya, said, 'Had I been there, I would have paid them only as idle workers, and not, as the *baraita* says, "IN FULL." '"

Surely the *baraita* taught: SOMEONE WHO CARRIES A LOAD IS NOT LIKE SOMEONE WHO TRAVELS EMPTY-HANDED, AND SOMEONE WHO WORKS IS NOT LIKE SOMEONE WHO SITS AND IS IDLE.

Rav Chiyya did not hear the concluding portion of the *baraita.*

There are others who say that Rav Chiyya did hear the concluding portion of the *baraita* and that this is what Rav said: My uncle said: If I had been there, I would not have paid him anything at all, but you say that he should be paid as an idle worker.

This is a contradiction.

There is no contradiction. Rav Chiyya's opinion, that the worker should not be paid, refers to a case where the employer checked his land the previous evening to see that it was workable. The statement in the *baraita* refers to a case where the employer did not check his land the previous evening.

Just as Rava said: If someone hired workers for digging, and it rained and filled the field with water, if he checked his land the previous evening, the loss is the workers'. If he did not check his field the previous evening, the loss is the employer's, and he must pay them as idle workers.

This is just as Rava said: If someone hired workers for irrigation, and it rained, the loss is the workers'. If the river overflowed, the loss is the employer's and he must give them their wages as idle workers.

And Rava said: If someone hired workers for irrigation, and the river from which the workers took the water stopped flowing in the middle of the day, if it doesn't often stop flowing, the loss is the workers'. If it frequently stops flowing, if the workers are from that locality, the loss is the workers'. If they are not from that locality, the loss is the employer's.

And Rava said: If someone hired people to do work, and the work was finished in the middle of the day, if the employer has other work to assign them that is easier than the work for which they were hired, he may give it to them. If it is equal to the work for which they were hired, he may give it to them. If it is harder than the work for which they were hired, he may not assign it to them and must pay them their wages in full.

Why should they be paid in full? Let him pay them as idle workers.

When Rava said this, he was referring to the porters of Mechoza, who become weak if they do not work.

Bava Metzia 75b

Mishnah: **IF SOMEONE HIRED AN ASS DRIVER OR A WAGON DRIVER TO BRING POLES OR FLUTES FOR A WEDDING OR A FUNERAL, OR IF SOMEONE HIRED WORKERS TO BRING HIS FLAX OUT OF THE STEEPING POND, OR FOR ANY JOB WHERE THE EMPLOYER WOULD SUFFER A LOSS IF THE CONTRACT WERE BROKEN, THEN IF THE WORKERS RETRACT AND THERE ARE NO OTHER WORKERS AVAILABLE TO DO THE JOB, HE MAY HIRE OTHER WORKERS AT THEIR EXPENSE OR HE MAY DECEIVE THEM.**

Bava Metzia 76b

Gemara: **IN THE CASE OF WHERE AN EMPLOYER WILL SUFFER A LOSS IF WORKERS BREAK A CONTRACT, HE MAY HIRE OTHER WORKERS AT THEIR EXPENSE OR HE MAY DECEIVE THEM. HOW MAY HE DECEIVE THEM? HE MAY SAY TO THEM: I PROMISED TO PAY YOU A *SELA*. COME AND TAKE TWO.**

AND HOW HIGH MAY HE GO TO HIRE OTHER WORKERS AT THEIR EXPENSE? UP TO FORTY OR FIFTY *ZUZ*.

UNDER WHAT CIRCUMSTANCES DOES THIS APPLY? WHEN THERE ARE NO OTHER WORKERS AVAILABLE THERE TO HIRE AND HE HAS TO HIRE FROM ANOTHER LOCALITY. BUT IF THERE ARE OTHER WORKERS AVAILABLE IN THAT LOCALITY, AND THE WORKERS WHO RETRACTED SAID TO HIM, "GO AND HIRE FROM AMONG THEM," THEN HE MUST HIRE FROM AMONG THEM, AND HE HAS GROUNDS ONLY FOR RESENTMENT.

Chapter Two

Quitting Before a Job Is Completed

Bava Metzia 76b

הַשּׁוֹכֵר אֶת הָאוּמָנִין וְהִטְעוּ אֶת בַּעַל הַבַּיִת, אוֹ בַּעַל הַבַּיִת הִטְעָה אוֹתָן, אֵין לָהֶם זֶה עַל זֶה אֶלָּא תַּרְעוֹמֶת.

בַּמֶּה דְּבָרִים אֲמוּרִים? שֶׁלֹּא הָלְכוּ, אֲבָל הָלְכוּ חַמָּרִים וְלֹא מָצְאוּ תְּבוּאָה, פּוֹעֲלִין וּמָצְאוּ שָׂדֶה כְּשֶׁהִיא לַחָה, נוֹתֵן לָהֶן שְׂכָרָן מְשֻׁלָּם. אֲבָל אֵינוֹ דוֹמֶה הַבָּא טָעוּן לַבָּא רֵיקָן, עוֹשֶׂה מְלָאכָה לְיוֹשֵׁב וּבָטֵל.

בַּמֶּה דְּבָרִים אֲמוּרִים? שֶׁלֹּא הִתְחִילוּ בִּמְלָאכָה. אֲבָל הִתְחִילוּ בִּמְלָאכָה, שָׁמִין לָהֶן מַה שֶּׁעָשׂוּ. כֵּיצַד? קִבְּלוּ קָמָה לִקְצוֹר בִּשְׁנֵי סְלָעִים, קָצְרוּ חֶצְיָהּ וְהִנִּיחוּ חֶצְיָהּ, בֶּגֶד לֶאֱרוֹג בִּשְׁנֵי סְלָעִים, אָרְגוּ חֶצְיוֹ וְהִנִּיחוּ חֶצְיוֹ, שָׁמִין לָהֶן אֶת מַה שֶּׁעָשׂוּ. הָיָה יָפֶה שִׁשָּׁה דִינָרִים, נוֹתֵן לָהֶן סֶלַע, אוֹ יִגְמְרוּ מְלַאכְתָּן וְיִטְּלוּ שְׁנֵי סְלָעִים. וְאִם סֶלַע, נוֹתֵן לָהֶם סֶלַע.

רַבִּי דוֹסָא אוֹמֵר: שָׁמִין לָהֶן מַה שֶּׁעָתִיד לְהֵעָשׂוֹת. הָיָה יָפֶה שִׁשָּׁה דִינָרִים, נוֹתֵן לָהֶם שֶׁקֶל, אוֹ יִגְמְרוּ מְלַאכְתָּן וְיִטְּלוּ שְׁנֵי סְלָעִים. וְאִם סֶלַע, נוֹתֵן לָהֶם סֶלַע.

Up to this point, the Gemara has dealt with the following cases:

1. Before the worker went to his job, either the employer or the employee broke the employment contract.

2. The contract was broken after the worker arrived at the place of employment but before any work was performed.

3. The worker finished the job before his workday was ended.

The Gemara now deals with the case of a worker who begins working but quits before his job is completed. This case is found in the continuation of the *baraita* previously cited: **IF SOMEONE HIRED ARTISANS AND THEY MISLED THE EMPLOYER, OR THE EMPLOYER MISLED THEM, THE ONE WHO WAS MISLED HAS GROUNDS ONLY FOR RESENTMENT AGAINST THE OTHER.**

UNDER WHAT CIRCUMSTANCES DOES THIS RULING APPLY? WHEN THEY DID NOT GO TO THE PLACE OF WORK. BUT IF ASS DRIVERS WENT AND DID NOT FIND PRODUCE TO HAUL, OR IF WORKERS WENT AND FOUND THAT THE FIELD WAS WATERLOGGED, THEN THE EMPLOYER MUST GIVE THEM THEIR WAGES IN FULL. BUT SOMEONE WHO CARRIES A LOAD IS NOT LIKE SOMEONE WHO TRAVELS EMPTY-HANDED, AND SOMEONE WHO WORKS IS NOT LIKE SOMEONE WHO SITS AND IS IDLE.

UNDER WHAT CIRCUMSTANCES DOES THIS RULING APPLY? WHEN THEY HAVE NOT BEGUN TO WORK. BUT IF THEY BEGAN TO WORK, WE CALCULATE THE VALUE OF WHAT THEY HAVE ACCOMPLISHED. HOW SO? IF THEY AGREED TO CUT STANDING CORN FOR TWO *SELAS* [eight *dinars*], AND THEY REAPED HALF OF IT AND LEFT HALF OF IT, OR IF A TAILOR AGREED TO WEAVE A GARMENT FOR TWO *SELAS* AND HE WOVE HALF OF IT AND LEFT HALF OF IT, WE CALCULATE THE VALUE OF WHAT THEY ACCOMPLISHED. IF WHAT THEY ACCOMPLISHED WAS WORTH SIX *DINARS*, HE GIVES THEM A *SELA* [four *dinars*], OR THEY MAY FINISH THEIR WORK AND RECEIVE TWO *SELAS*. BUT IF WHAT THEY ACCOMPLISHED WAS WORTH A *SELA*, THEN HE GIVES THEM A *SELA*.

If the worker quits after finishing half the job, the *baraita* rules that the worker receives half the contract wage. And even if the price of labor rose, and what the worker accomplished was worth six *dinars*, he still receives only four *dinars*, half the contract wage.

Anonymous rulings in a *baraita* are considered authoritative. They represented the majority opinion of the Rabbis. A ruling recorded in the name of an individual Sage is a minority view, deemed important enough to be preserved.

The Gemara's citation of the *baraita* continues by presenting a minority opinion: **RABBI DOSA SAYS: WE CALCULATE THE COST OF WHAT REMAINS TO BE DONE TO FINISH THE JOB. IF WHAT REMAINS TO BE DONE WILL COST SIX** *DINARS*, **HE GIVES THEM A** *SHEKEL* [two *dinars*], **OR THEY MAY FINISH THEIR WORK AND RECEIVE TWO** *SELAS*. **BUT IF WHAT REMAINS TO BE DONE WILL COST A** *SELA*, **HE GIVES THEM A** *SELA*.

Rabbi Dosa disputes the majority in a fundamental way. He doesn't calculate what the worker has accomplished; he calculates what it will cost the employer to get the rest of the job done. If wages have gone up and it will cost the employer more than one-half of the original contract wage to have the job completed, Rabbi Dosa will have the employer deduct that extra cost from the worker's pay.

The majority of the Rabbis, on the other hand, maintained that an employee who quits before completing his contract should not be penalized in this way. He should be paid proportionately, for that part of the work that he completed.

Scholars have long debated the reason for the inclusion of minority views in *mishnayot* and *baraitot*. Some have said that minority views were included to reinforce the majority rulings by showing what opinions had been overruled. Others have maintained that minority views were included because the law was still in flux, and a record of the debates could aid future generations in their study of the law.

One *sela* = two *shekels* = four *dinars*.

Rabbi Dosa (ben Horkinas) was a prominent Sage during the first century C.E. He lived a long life, participating in discussions of law before the destruction of the Temple and still being active during the time of the deliberations at Yavneh after its fall. His opinions are cited in a few *mishnayot* and in numerous *baraitot*.

What's Your Opinion?

Should someone who quits before finishing the work he promised to do be penalized if having the job completed will entail additional cost for the employer? Is an employee bound to a contract in the same way that an employer is? Should there be instances when an employee should be allowed to break a contract in order to take advantage of an opportunity to better himself?

Consider These Cases

Marla had a summer job at a restaurant in Glencoe, Illinois. In the middle of the summer she received a call from the Union Institute camp in Oconomowoc, Wisconsin. A counselor had left, and the camp was in dire need of her services in a position for which she was highly qualified.

Marla sought the advice of her parents. Her father said that she had faithfully promised the restaurant owner that she would work for him the entire summer. He said that she should not break a solemn commitment. Her mother said that serving as a camp counselor would be a mitzvah and that it would be good for her to be in a Jewish environment at camp.

What should Marla do?

Rabbi Cohen was given a five-year contract at Beth Israel Congregation, which he enthusiastically accepted. He did an outstanding job and was loved by the congregation members. He was happy at Beth Israel and had no intention of leaving, but after two years, he was offered a position at a larger congregation in the community where his parents and his wife's parents lived. For him it was an ideal opportunity.
Should Rabbi Cohen leave Beth Israel with three years still remaining on his contract? Should Beth Israel allow Rabbi Cohen to break his contract without a penalty?

REVIEWING THE TEXT

Bava Metzia 76b

Gemara: **IF SOMEONE HIRED ARTISANS AND THEY MISLED THE EMPLOYER, OR THE EMPLOYER MISLED THEM, THE ONE WHO WAS MISLED HAS GROUNDS ONLY FOR RESENTMENT AGAINST THE OTHER.**

UNDER WHAT CIRCUMSTANCES DOES THIS RULING APPLY? WHEN THEY DID NOT GO TO THE PLACE OF WORK. BUT IF ASS DRIVERS WENT AND DID NOT FIND PRODUCE TO HAUL, OR IF WORKERS WENT AND FOUND THAT THE FIELD WAS WATERLOGGED, THEN THE EMPLOYER MUST GIVE THEM THEIR WAGES IN FULL. BUT SOMEONE WHO CARRIES A LOAD IS NOT LIKE SOMEONE WHO TRAVELS EMPTY-HANDED, AND SOMEONE WHO WORKS IS NOT LIKE SOMEONE WHO SITS AND IS IDLE.

UNDER WHAT CIRCUMSTANCES DOES THIS RULING APPLY? WHEN THEY HAVE NOT BEGUN TO WORK. BUT IF THEY BEGAN TO WORK, WE CALCULATE THE VALUE OF WHAT THEY HAVE ACCOMPLISHED. HOW SO? IF THEY AGREED TO CUT STANDING CORN FOR TWO *SELAS*, AND THEY REAPED HALF OF IT AND LEFT HALF OF IT, OR IF A TAILOR AGREED TO WEAVE A GARMENT FOR TWO *SELAS*, AND HE WOVE HALF OF IT AND LEFT HALF OF IT, WE CALCULATE THE VALUE OF WHAT THEY ACCOMPLISHED. IF WHAT THEY ACCOMPLISHED WAS WORTH SIX *DINARS*, HE GIVES THEM A *SELA*, OR THEY MAY FINISH THEIR WORK AND RECEIVE TWO *SELAS*. BUT IF WHAT THEY ACCOMPLISHED WAS WORTH A *SELA*, THEN HE GIVES THEM A *SELA*.

RABBI DOSA SAYS: WE CALCULATE THE COST OF WHAT REMAINS TO BE DONE TO FINISH THE JOB. IF WHAT REMAINS TO BE DONE WILL COST SIX *DINARS*, HE GIVES THEM A *SHEKEL*, OR THEY MAY FINISH THEIR WORK AND RECEIVE TWO *SELAS*. BUT IF WHAT REMAINS TO BE DONE WILL COST A *SELA*, HE GIVES THEM A *SELA*.

Chapter Three

How Long Is the Workday?

Bava Metzia 83a

הַשּׂוֹכֵר אֶת הַפּוֹעֲלִים וְאָמַר לָהֶם לְהַשְׁכִּים וּלְהַעֲרִיב. מָקוֹם שֶׁנָּהֲגוּ שֶׁלֹּא לְהַשְׁכִּים וְשֶׁלֹּא לְהַעֲרִיב, אֵינוֹ רַשַּׁאי לְכוֹפָן. מָקוֹם שֶׁנָּהֲגוּ לָזוּן, יָזוּן, לְסַפֵּק בִּמְתִיקָה, יְסַפֵּק, הַכֹּל כְּמִנְהַג הַמְּדִינָה.

Mishnah: **IF SOMEONE HIRED WORKERS AND TOLD THEM TO COME EARLY OR TO STAY LATE, IN A PLACE WHERE IT IS CUSTOMARY NOT TO COME EARLY OR TO STAY LATE, HE MAY NOT FORCE THEM. IN A PLACE WHERE IT IS CUSTOMARY TO FEED THEM, HE MUST FEED THEM, TO PROVIDE THEM WITH DESSERT, HE MUST PROVIDE IT. EVERYTHING IS IN ACCORDANCE WITH LOCAL CUSTOM.**

Bava Metzia 83a-b

פְּשִׁיטָא.

לָא צְרִיכָא, דִּטְפָא לְהוּ אַאַגְרַיְיהוּ. מַהוּ דְּתֵימָא, אָמַר לְהוּ: הָא דִּטְפַאי לְכוּ אַאַגְרַיְיכוּ, אַדַּעְתָּא דִּמְקַדְמִיתוּ וּמְחַשְׁכִיתוּ בַּהֲדַאי. קָא מַשְׁמַע לָן דַּאֲמָרוּ לֵיהּ: הַאי דִּטְפַת לָן, אַדַּעְתָּא דְּעָבְדִינַן לָךְ עֲבִידְתָּא שַׁפִּירְתָּא.

אָמַר רֵישׁ לָקִישׁ: פּוֹעֵל, בִּכְנִיסָתוֹ, מִשֶּׁלּוֹ, בִּיצִיאָתוֹ, מִשֶּׁל בַּעַל הַבַּיִת, שֶׁנֶּאֱמַר "תִּזְרַח הַשֶּׁמֶשׁ יֵאָסֵפוּן וְאֶל מְעוֹנֹתָם יִרְבָּצוּן יֵצֵא אָדָם לְפָעֳלוֹ וְלַעֲבֹדָתוֹ עֲדֵי עָרֶב".

וְלִיחֲזֵי הֵיכִי נְהִיגִי.

בְּעִיר חֲדָשָׁה.

וְנֶיחֲזֵי מֵהֵיכָא קָא אָתוּ.

בִּנְקוּטָאֵי. אִיבָּעֵית אֵימָא, דַּאֲמַר לְהוּ: דְּאַגְרִיתוּ לִי כְּפוֹעֵל דְּאוֹרַיְיתָא.

The Gemara states: **This is obvious.** Since the Mishnah stated that everything was in accordance with local custom, it was obvious that the employer was not allowed to force them to come early or to stay late when local custom dictated otherwise. Why then was it necessary for the Mishnah to spell it out?

The Gemara explains: **No. It was necessary to include this ruling for a case where the employer paid higher than normal wages. One might have thought that the employer could say to the workers: I added to your wages on condition that you would come early and stay late with me. The ruling in the Mishnah was thus necessary because the workers could say to the employer: You added to our wages on condition that we would do especially good work for you.**

The Gemara thus rules that the length of the working day is governed by local custom as opposed to the wishes of an individual employer.

The Gemara continues: **Resh Lakish said: When a worker returns home after his day of work, he returns on his own time; when he leaves his home in the morning to go to work, he leaves on the time of his employer, as it is said, "The sun rises, the animals gather themselves together and lay themselves down in their dens. Man goes out to his work and to his labor until the evening"** (Ps.104:22-23).

Rabbi Simeon ben Lakish, commonly known as Resh Lakish, was one of the more romantic figures among the Sages. He was reputed to be a man of great courage and physical strength and was said to have been, for a period of time, a Roman gladiator. Resh Lakish was one of the most eminent Palestinian Sages of the third century. The Talmud records many controversies between him and his brother-in-law, Rabbi Yochanan.

Resh Lakish uses a verse from Psalms to expound his teaching about when a worker sets out for work in the morning and when he returns home in the evening. The verse teaches that at daybreak, man sets out for work. Thus if the employer is paying the worker for the day, he is already paying for the morning trip to work. But if the worker labors until nightfall, then he is on his own during his commute home.

The Gemara then raises an objection to Resh Lakish's statement: **But let us see what is the local custom.** If everything is in accordance with local custom, then what need is there for Resh Lakish's ruling?

The Gemara responds: **In a new town.** Resh Lakish's ruling would be useful in a new town where no local custom exists.

Again the Gemara objects: **Then let us see from where they have come.** The custom of the town from which the inhabitants have come should prevail.

The Gemara responds that Resh Lakish's ruling could refer to: **a place where the inhabitants have gathered from many different places or, if you prefer, to a place where an employer said to the workers: "You are hired by me according to Torah law."**

What's Your Opinion?

Later commentators have said that an employer may stipulate the terms of employment when he hires his workers, and if the workers agree, then the stipulated terms remain in force and take precedence over local custom. According to this view, the Mishnah's statement, "everything is in accordance with local custom," applied only where no advance stipulations were made. Do you agree with the view of these commentators? If a worker agrees, should an employer be allowed to specify any hours of employment he wishes? Should local custom have a role in determining working conditions, or should the economic needs of a business always take precedence?

REVIEWING THE TEXT

Bava Metzia 83a

Mishnah: **IF SOMEONE HIRED WORKERS AND TOLD THEM TO COME EARLY OR TO STAY LATE, IN A PLACE WHERE IT IS CUSTOMARY NOT TO COME EARLY OR TO STAY LATE, HE MAY NOT FORCE THEM. IN A PLACE WHERE IT IS CUSTOMARY TO FEED THEM, HE MUST FEED THEM, TO PROVIDE THEM WITH DESSERT, HE MUST PROVIDE IT. EVERYTHING IS IN ACCORDANCE WITH LOCAL CUSTOM.**

Bava Metzia 83a-b

Gemara: **This is obvious.**

No. It was necessary to include this ruling for a case where the employer paid higher than normal wages. One might have thought that the employer could say to the workers: I added to your wages on condition that you would come early and stay late with me. The ruling in the Mishnah was thus necessary because the workers could say to the employer: You added to our wages on condition that we would do especially good work for you.

Resh Lakish said: When a worker returns home after his day of work, he returns on his own time; when he leaves his home in the morning to go to work, he leaves on the time of his employer, as it is said, "The sun rises, the animals gather

themselves together and lay themselves down in their dens. Man goes out to his work and to his labor until the evening."

But let us see what is the local custom.

In a new town.

Then let us see from where they have come.

A place where the inhabitants have gathered from many different places or, if you prefer, to a place where an employer said to the workers: "You are hired by me according to Torah law."

Chapter Four

Eating at the Employer's Expense

Bava Metzia 87a-b

וְאֵלּוּ אוֹכְלִין מִן הַתּוֹרָה: הָעוֹשֶׂה בִּמְחוּבָּר לַקַּרְקַע בִּשְׁעַת
גְּמַר מְלָאכָה, וּבְתָלוּשׁ מִן הַקַּרְקַע עַד שֶׁלֹּא נִגְמְרָה מְלַאכְתּוֹ,
וּבְדָבָר שֶׁגִּידּוּלוֹ מִן הָאָרֶץ.
וְאֵלּוּ שֶׁאֵין אוֹכְלִים: הָעוֹשֶׂה בִּמְחוּבָּר לַקַּרְקַע בְּשָׁעָה שֶׁאֵין
גְּמַר מְלָאכָה, וּבְתָלוּשׁ מִן הַקַּרְקַע מֵאַחַר שֶׁנִּגְמְרָה מְלַאכְתּוֹ,
וּבְדָבָר שֶׁאֵין גִּידוּלוֹ מִן הָאָרֶץ.

The Torah teaches: "When you enter your neighbor's vineyard,
you may eat as many grapes as you wish, until you are full, but
you must not put any in your vessel. When you enter another
man's field of standing grain, you may pluck ears with your hand;
but you must not put a sickle to your neighbor's grain" (Deut.
23:25-26). The Rabbis explained these verses to mean that
workers, while they were on the job, could eat from their
employer's produce.

Mishnah: **AND THESE EAT BY TORAH LAW: SOMEONE WHO
WORKS WITH PRODUCE ATTACHED TO THE GROUND AT THE
TIME THE WORK IS BEING FINISHED, OR WITH PRODUCE
DETACHED FROM THE GROUND BEFORE WORK ON IT IS
FINISHED, AND ONLY WITH SOMETHING WHOSE GROWTH IS
FROM THE EARTH.**

BUT THESE DO NOT EAT: SOMEONE WHO WORKS WITH PRODUCE ATTACHED TO THE GROUND WHEN THE WORK HAS NOT BEEN FINISHED, OR WITH PRODUCE DETACHED FROM THE GROUND AFTER WORK ON IT HAS BEEN FINISHED, OR WITH SOMETHING WHOSE GROWTH IS NOT FROM THE EARTH.

According to the Mishnah, someone whose job is to pick plums would be allowed to eat of the plums, for the plums are attached to the ground and, since they are being picked, their work is finished. But someone whose job is to spray the plum trees would not be allowed to eat of them because their work is not yet finished.

Also, someone whose job is to take the dates from the baskets and place them in shipping crates would be allowed to eat of them because they are detached fruit whose work is not yet finished, but someone who brings the packed crates to the market would not be allowed to eat of them because they are detached fruit whose work is finished.

Furthermore, someone who milks the cows or collects eggs from the hens would not be allowed to drink the milk or eat the eggs because their growth is not from the earth.

What's Your Opinion?

Is it reasonable that the workers may eat only produce that grows from the ground? Is it reasonable that they may eat attached produce only if it is ripe and ready to be harvested and may eat detached produce only if it is not completely finished?

Consider This Case

Jerome is a member of the Board of Directors of Healthy Foods. Healthy owns some 400 supermarkets throughout the country. At a directors meeting, a proposal has been made to allow supermarket employees to eat Healthy's fruits and salads during lunch or dinner breaks at no charge.

Jerome is uncertain how to vote on this proposal. He thinks that giving the workers such a benefit will be appreciated by them and might help to build morale and loyalty among them. On the other hand, he is concerned about giving away produce that is ready to be sold to paying customers.

How would you vote were you a member of the Board of Directors? Explain your view.

Bava Metzia 91b

הָיָה עוֹשֶׂה בִּתְאֵנִים, לֹא יֹאכַל בַּעֲנָבִים, בַּעֲנָבִים, לֹא יֹאכַל בִּתְאֵנִים. אֲבָל מוֹנֵעַ אֶת עַצְמוֹ עַד שֶׁמַּגִּיעַ לִמְקוֹם יָפוֹת וְאוֹכֵל.

Mishnah: **IF A WORKER WAS PICKING FIGS, HE MAY NOT EAT GRAPES. IF HE WAS PICKING GRAPES, HE MAY NOT EAT FIGS. BUT HE MAY RESTRAIN HIMSELF UNTIL HE REACHES A PLACE OF CHOICE FRUIT AND THEN HE MAY EAT.**

The law of the Torah, as interpreted by the Rabbis, allowed a worker to eat of the fruit he was harvesting. But the Mishnah makes it clear that the law allows the worker to eat only of the fruit on which he is working and not any other fruit in his employer's fields.

Bava Metzia 91b

עוֹשֶׂה בְּגֶפֶן זֶה, מַהוּ שֶׁיֹּאכַל בְּגֶפֶן אַחֵר? מִמִּין שֶׁאַתָּה נוֹתֵן לְכֵלָיו שֶׁל בַּעַל הַבַּיִת בָּעֵינָן, וְהָא אִיכָּא, אוֹ דִּלְמָא מִמַּה שֶׁאַתָּה נוֹתֵן לְכֵלָיו שֶׁל בַּעַל הַבַּיִת בָּעֵינָן, וְהָא לֵיכָּא?

וְאִם תִּמְצֵי לוֹמַר: עוֹשֶׂה בְּגֶפֶן זֶה לֹא יֹאכַל בְּגֶפֶן אַחֵר, שׁוֹר בִּמְחוּבָּר הֵיכִי אֲכִיל?

אָמַר רַב שֵׁישָׁא בְּרֵיהּ דְּרַב אִידִי: בִּשְׂרָכָא.

The Gemara then raises the following question: **If he is working on one vine, may he eat from another vine? Does the Mishnah mean that he may eat only of the kind of fruit that he is putting into his employer's utensils, or does it mean that he may eat only of the particular vine that he is putting into his employer's utensils?**

By observing the ox, the Gemara reasons that one may eat from a vine other than the one he is working on. **If you say that if he is working on one vine, he may not eat of another vine, how could an ox working on what is attached to the ground eat?**

If an ox pulls a wagon containing the grapes that are being harvested, the ox's head is probably next to a vine other than the one being harvested. Surely one would not want to prevent an ox from eating from a nearby vine. This then would suggest that just as an ox may eat from a vine other than the one being harvested, so a worker should be allowed to eat from a vine other than the one he is working on.

Rav Shesha the son of Rav Idi was a fourth-century Babylonian *Amora*.

However, the Gemara rejects this argument for: **Rav Shesha the son of Rav Idi said: There are long branches.** The ox may, indeed, be able to eat from the same vine as the one being worked on, so nothing may be learned from the case of the ox to help answer the Gemara's question.

Bava Metzia 91b

אֲבָל מוֹנֵעַ אֶת עַצְמוֹ עַד שֶׁמַּגִּיעַ לְמְקוֹם הַיָּפוֹת וְאוֹכֵל. וְאִי אָמְרַתְּ עוֹשֶׂה בְּגֶפֶן זֶה אוֹכֵל בְּגֶפֶן אַחֵר, נֵיזִיל וְנֵיתֵי וְנֵיכוֹל. הָתָם, מִשּׁוּם בִּיטּוּל מְלָאכָה.

The Gemara then turns to the Mishnah to show that the worker may *not* eat of any vine other than the one he is harvesting: **BUT HE MAY RESTRAIN HIMSELF UNTIL HE REACHES A PLACE OF CHOICE FRUIT AND THEN HE MAY EAT. Now if you say that if**

he is working on one vine, he may eat of another vine, then he need not restrain himself. He may simply go to the other vine, bring some grapes to the place where he is working, and eat.

Since the Mishnah says that in order to eat from a particularly sweet vine, the worker needs to restrain himself until he gets there, it proves that he may eat only from that vine upon which he is working.

But the Gemara rejects this argument as well: **The rule is stated there, in the Mishnah, because of loss of work.** The reason that the worker has to restrain himself if he wants to eat from a particular vine is because the worker is not allowed to take time off from his job of harvesting to go to another vine and bring back his favorite grapes. Thus we cannot conclude from the Mishnah that the worker is forbidden to partake of another vine.

The Gemara raises a question. May a worker eat from a vine other than the one on which he is working? It cites the case of an ox to prove that he may, indeed, eat from another vine. This proof, however, is rejected. Then the Gemara cites the Mishnah to prove that he may *not* eat from another vine. This proof is also rejected. The Gemara, in fact, does not answer the question that it raised. This may indicate that the editors of the Gemara were more interested in preserving the analysis of the law through reasoned arguments than they were in reaching legal decisions.

What's Your Opinion?

What should the rule be? What did the biblical law intend? Should a worker be allowed to eat from any fruit in the employer's field? any fruit of the type being harvested? only from the vine or tree from which the worker is picking?

Consider This Case

Bayside Grapes is one of the largest vineyard owners in northern California. During the harvest season they employ about 200 workers. The workers are allowed to eat as many grapes as they wish while they are on the job, but a problem has come up in that the workers like to do most of their eating from the prime vines rather than from the vines on which they are working. Bayside's owners find that a large percentage of their best grapes are gone in the fields and never get to the crates for shipment to market.

Do you think that Bayside should restrict eating to the actual vines from which a worker is picking? Explain your view.

מַעֲשֶׂה בְּרַבִּי יוֹחָנָן בֶּן מַתְיָא שֶׁאָמַר לִבְנוֹ: צֵא שְׂכוֹר לָנוּ פּוֹעֲלִין. הָלַךְ וּפָסַק לָהֶם מְזוֹנוֹת. וּכְשֶׁבָּא אֵצֶל אָבִיו, אָמַר לוֹ: בְּנִי, אֲפִילוּ אִם אַתָּה עוֹשֶׂה לָהֶם כִּסְעוּדַת שְׁלֹמֹה בְּשַׁעְתּוֹ לֹא יָצָאתָ יְדֵי חוֹבָתְךָ עִמָּהֶן, שֶׁהֵן בְּנֵי אַבְרָהָם יִצְחָק וְיַעֲקֹב. אֶלָּא, עַד שֶׁלֹּא יַתְחִילוּ בִּמְלָאכָה צֵא וֶאֱמוֹר לָהֶם: עַל מְנָת שֶׁאֵין לָכֶם עָלַי אֶלָּא פַּת וְקִטְנִית בִּלְבָד.

רַבָּן שִׁמְעוֹן בֶּן גַּמְלִיאֵל אוֹמֵר: לֹא הָיָה צָרִיךְ לוֹמַר, הַכֹּל כְּמִנְהַג הַמְּדִינָה.

Mishnah: **RABBI YOCHANAN BEN MATYA ONCE SAID TO HIS SON: GO OUT AND HIRE WORKERS FOR US. HE WENT AND PROMISED THEM FOOD. BUT WHEN HE CAME TO HIS FATHER, HIS FATHER SAID TO HIM: MY SON, EVEN IF YOU MAKE A MEAL FOR THEM LIKE SOLOMON'S FEAST IN HIS TIME, YOU HAVE NOT FULFILLED YOUR OBLIGATION TOWARD THEM, FOR THEY ARE CHILDREN OF ABRAHAM, ISAAC, AND JACOB. RATHER, BEFORE THEY BEGIN WORK, GO OUT AND SAY TO THEM: ON CONDITION THAT YOU HAVE NO CLAIM ON ME EXCEPT FOR BREAD AND BEANS.**

RABBAN SIMEON BEN GAMALIEL SAYS: RABBI YOCHANAN BEN MATYA DID NOT NEED TO SAY THIS, FOR EVERYTHING IS IN ACCORDANCE WITH LOCAL CUSTOM.

Rabbi Yochanan ben Matya was concerned that the food his son promised the workers might be interpreted by them as a large feast. Rabban Simeon ben Gamaliel said that Rabbi Yochanan need not have been concerned, for the workers would have expected only such food as is customary in the locality.

Bava Metzia 87a

אָמַר לֵיה רַב אַחָא בְּרֵיה דְּרַב יוֹסֵף לְרַב חִסְדָּא: פַּת קִטְנִית תְּנַן, אוֹ פַּת וְקִטְנִית תְּנַן? אֲמַר לֵיה: הָאֱלֹהִים, צְרִיכָה וי"ו כִּי מוֹרְדְיָא דְלִבְרוֹת.

רַבָּן שִׁמְעוֹן בֶּן גַּמְלִיאֵל אוֹמֵר אֵינוֹ צָרִיךְ הַכֹּל כְּמִנְהַג הַמְּדִינָה. "הַכֹּל" לְאַתּוּיֵי מַאי?

לְאַתּוּיֵי הָא דִּתְנַן: הַשּׂוֹכֵר אֶת הַפּוֹעֵל וְאָמַר לוֹ כְּאֶחָד וְכִשְׁנַיִם מִבְּנֵי הָעִיר, נוֹתֵן לוֹ כְּפָחוֹת שֶׁבַּשְּׂכִירוֹת. דִּבְרֵי רַבִּי יְהוֹשֻׁעַ, וַחֲכָמִים אוֹמְרִים: מְשַׁמְּנִין בֵּינֵיהֶם.

Gemara: **Rav Acha the son of Rav Joseph said to Rav Chisda: Did we learn bread made of beans or did we learn BREAD AND BEANS? Rav Chisda responded: The *vav*, meaning AND, should be prominent like the rudder of a ship.**

The Gemara then inquires: **When Rabbi Simeon ben Gamaliel said that EVERYTHING IS IN ACCORDANCE WITH LOCAL CUSTOM, what was the significance of the word EVERYTHING?**

Its significance was to teach what we have learned in a *baraita*: IF SOMEONE HIRED A WORKER AND SAID TO HIM: I WILL PAY YOU LIKE THE WAGES OF ONE OR TWO OF THE TOWNSPEOPLE, HE MAY PAY HIM AT THE LOWEST WAGE. THESE ARE THE WORDS OF RABBI JOSHUA. BUT THE SAGES SAY THAT WE MUST PAY AT THE AVERAGE WAGE AMONG THE TOWNSPEOPLE.

There was a difference of opinion as to what it meant to pay workers according to local wage scales. Rabbi Joshua maintained that if an employer found one or two instances where local workers were receiving a low rate of pay, the employer could follow that example and be satisfied that he was following local custom. The majority of the Rabbis were of the opinion, however, that finding one or two examples of wage payments was not sufficient. It was necessary to take an average to determine what was the true local custom.

Rav Acha the son of Rav Joseph and Rav Chisda were Babylonian *Amoraim* during the end of the third century and the start of the fourth century. Rav Chisda is one of the most frequently mentioned Sages of the Talmud. Early in his life he was poor but later became wealthy. In the last decade of his life, he became head of the academy at Sura. In addition to his great scholarship, he was known for his charitable works. When the academy at Sura fell into disrepair, he had it rebuilt at his own expense.

Rabbi Joshua (ben Chananiah) was a student of Rabbi Yochanan ben Zakkai during Second Temple times and became one of the foremost rabbinic authorities after the fall of the Temple. He was an advocate for the views of the academy of Hillel, and his opinions generally prevailed among the Sages. In a dispute over the calendar with the head of the Sanhedrin, Rabban Gamaliel, Rabbi Joshua submitted to Rabban Gamaliel's authority, thus helping to maintain the unity of observances throughout the Jewish community. He is cited 160 times in the Mishnah.

What's Your Opinion?

If the law is to follow local custom, do you believe that an employer should be allowed to follow the rate of the lower-paying local establishments, or should he be required to pay according to average town wages? Do you believe that the requirement to follow local custom is a good idea, or should someone be allowed to pay any wage that a worker will accept?

Consider This Case

Border Grape Farm engages in a highly competitive business. At the grape-picking season, legal immigrants from Mexico offer to work for half of what U.S. workers demand. Is it right for Border Grape Farm to hire the immigrants?

Bava Metzia 92a

אוֹכֵל פּוֹעֵל קִישׁוּת אֲפִילוּ בְּדִינָר, כּוֹתֶבֶת וַאֲפִילוּ בְּדִינָר. רַבִּי אֶלְעָזָר חִסְמָא אוֹמֵר: לֹא יֹאכַל פּוֹעֵל יָתֵר עַל שְׂכָרוֹ, וַחֲכָמִים מַתִּירִין. אֲבָל מְלַמְּדִין אֶת הָאָדָם שֶׁלֹּא יְהֵא רַעַבְתָן וִיהֵא סוֹתֵם אֶת הַפֶּתַח בְּפָנָיו.

חֲכָמִים הַיְינוּ תַּנָּא קַמָּא. אִיכָּא בֵּינַיְיהוּ "אֲבָל מְלַמְּדִין". לְתַנָּא קַמָּא לֵית לֵיהּ "מְלַמְּדִין", לְרַבָּנָן אִית לְהוּ "מְלַמְּדִין". אִיבָּעֵית אֵימָא: אִיכָּא בֵּינַיְיהוּ דְרַב אַסִי. דְּאָמַר רַב אַסִי: אֲפִילוּ לֹא שְׂכָרוֹ אֶלָּא לִבְצוֹר אֶשְׁכּוֹל אֶחָד, אוֹכְלוֹ.

Rabbi Eleazar Chisma lived in the middle of the second century and was among the first students of Rabbi Akiva.

Mishnah: **A WORKER MAY EAT A CUCUMBER EVEN IF IT COSTS AS MUCH AS A *DINAR*, OR A DATE EVEN IF IT COSTS AS MUCH AS A *DINAR*. RABBI ELEAZAR CHISMA SAYS: A WORKER MAY NOT EAT MORE THAN HIS WAGE. BUT THE SAGES PERMIT IT, BUT THEY TEACH A PERSON NOT TO BE A GLUTTON AND SHUT THE DOOR IN HIS OWN FACE.**

The Gemara points to the similarity between the Mishnah's first statement, listed anonymously, and its last statement, recorded in the name of the Sages. **Surely the Sages and the first _Tanna_ are of the same opinion.** That is, both statements allow the worker to eat as much as he wishes.

However, the Gemara points out: **There is a difference between the two opinions. The difference is BUT THEY TEACH A PERSON NOT TO BE A GLUTTON. The first _Tanna_ does not say anything about gluttony, whereas the Sages maintain that we should teach the worker not to be a glutton.**

The Gemara then suggests another difference between the views of the anonymous _Tanna_ and the Sages. **If you wish, you can say that the difference between them is their opinion regarding the following statement of Rav Assi: Even if he was hired to pick only one bunch of grapes, he may eat it.** The anonymous _Tanna_ is in agreement with Rav Assi's ruling, whereas the Sages, on grounds of gluttony, forbid a worker to eat all that he was hired to pick.

Rav Assi was a first-generation Babylonian _Amora_.

What's Your Opinion?

Is Rav Assi's extreme statement intended to point out that no limitation should be placed on the worker's right to eat? Is this a valid point? Should Rav Assi's statement be disputed on grounds of gluttony?

Consider This Case

Ernest works as a computer programmer at Clear Copy, Inc. His contract with Clear Copy states that he may make photocopies at no charge. Ernest takes classes at night and normally copies articles and materials for himself and all his classmates. On any given day he may make hundreds of copies. Is this all right, or should he be warned not to be a glutton and possibly shut the door in his own face?

אִיבָּעֵית אֵימָא: אִיכָּא בֵּינַיְיהוּ דְּרַב. דְּאָמַר רַב: מָצָאתִי
מְגִילַת סְתָרִים בֵּי רַבִּי חִיָּיא, וְכָתוּב בָּהּ: אִיסִי בֶּן יְהוּדָה
אוֹמֵר "כִּי תָבֹא בְּכֶרֶם רֵעֶךָ". בְּבִיאַת כָּל אָדָם הַכָּתוּב מְדַבֵּר.

וַאֲמַר רַב: לֹא שָׁבַק אִיסִי חַיֵּי לְכָל בְּרִיָּה.

אֲמַר רַב אַשִׁי: אֲמְרִיתָהּ לִשְׁמַעֲתָא קַמֵּיהּ דְּרַב כָּהֲנָא דִּלְמָא
בְּעוֹשִׂין בִּסְעוּדָתָם, דְּעָבְדוּ וְאָכְלוּ.

אֲמַר לִי: אֲפִילּוּ הָכִי, נִיחָא לֵיהּ לְאִינִישׁ לְאוֹגַר אֲגוּרֵי
וְנִיקְטְפֵיהּ לְפַרְדֵיסֵיהּ, וְלָא נֵיתוּ כּוּלֵּי עָלְמָא וְאָכְלוּ לֵיהּ.

Although written notes of the Sages' comments or interpretations were not taken during sessions of the academies, undoubtedly many scholars, in the privacy of their homes, kept records, for their own personal use, of the statements of their teachers and colleagues. Such a record must have been the secret scroll discovered in the house of Rav Chiyya.

Issi ben Judah was a *Tanna* who lived near the end of the second century. His teachings are found in many *baraitot*.

The Gemara then suggests a third difference between the views of the first *Tanna* and the Sages. **If you wish, you can say that the difference between them is their opinion regarding the following statement of Rav: I found a secret scroll in the house of Rabbi Chiyya in which it was written that Issi ben Judah commented on the verse, "When you enter your neighbor's vineyard, you may eat as many grapes as you wish, until you are full"** (Deut. 23:25), **and said: The verse refers not just to workers, but to any person who comes upon a vineyard.**

And Rav said: Issi would not allow any vineyard owner to survive.

Rav believed that Issi's interpretation of the biblical verse was untenable. The Torah, according to Rav, could not possibly have meant that any person could walk into any vineyard and help himself. No vineyard owner could survive if that were the case. According to this suggestion of the Gemara, then, the difference between the views of the first *Tanna* and the Sages was that the first *Tanna* agreed with Rav saying: "A *worker* may eat a cucumber," specifying that the law applied only to workers, whereas the Sages' statement, which did not explicitly mention workers, agreed with Issi.

Rav Ashi said: I reported this teaching to Rav Kahana and suggested to him: Perhaps Issi's statement applies to those who work for their meals, for they work and eat.

Rav Ashi suggested that Issi didn't mean that anyone could walk in and eat, but rather that anyone who was willing to work could walk in, work, and eat.

Rav Kahana replied to Rav Ashi: Even so, a person wants to choose those whom he will hire to harvest his orchard and not allow anyone to start working and eat from it.

Over the course of the generations, a number of Sages were named Rav Kahana. The Rav Kahana mentioned here was the one who lived near the end of the fourth century and was a teacher of Rav Ashi.

What's Your Opinion?

What is the meaning of the biblical verse, "When you enter your neighbor's vineyard, you may eat as many grapes as you wish, until you are full"? Even though the Torah's law didn't specify "workers," were the Rabbis right to interpret it to refer only to workers?

R E V I E W I N G   T H E   T E X T

Buva Metzia 87a-b

Mishnah: **AND THESE EAT BY TORAH LAW: SOMEONE WHO WORKS WITH PRODUCE ATTACHED TO THE GROUND AT THE TIME THE WORK IS BEING FINISHED, OR WITH PRODUCE DETACHED FROM THE GROUND BEFORE ITS WORK IS FINISHED, AND ONLY WITH SOMETHING WHOSE GROWTH IS FROM THE EARTH.**

BUT THESE DO NOT EAT: SOMEONE WHO WORKS WITH PRODUCE ATTACHED TO THE GROUND WHEN THE WORK IS NOT BEING FINISHED, OR WITH PRODUCE DETACHED FROM THE GROUND AFTER ITS WORK HAS BEEN FINISHED, OR WITH SOMETHING WHOSE GROWTH IS NOT FROM THE EARTH.

Mishnah: **IF A WORKER WAS PICKING FIGS, HE MAY NOT EAT GRAPES. IF HE WAS PICKING GRAPES, HE MAY NOT EAT FIGS. BUT HE MAY RESTRAIN HIMSELF UNTIL HE REACHES A PLACE OF CHOICE FRUIT AND THEN HE MAY EAT.**

Gemara: **If he is working on one vine, may he eat from another vine? Does the Mishnah mean that he may eat only of the kind of fruit that he is putting into his employer's utensils, or does it mean that he may eat only of the particular vine that he is putting into his employer's utensils?**

If you say that if he is working on one vine, he may not eat of another vine, how could an ox working on what is attached to the ground eat?

Rav Shesha the son of Rav Idi said: There are long branches.

BUT HE MAY RESTRAIN HIMSELF UNTIL HE REACHES A PLACE OF CHOICE FRUIT AND THEN HE MAY EAT. Now if you say that if he is working on one vine, he may eat of another vine, then he need not restrain himself. He may simply go to the other vine, bring some grapes to the place where he is working, and eat.

The rule is stated there, in the Mishnah, because of loss of work.

Mishnah: **RABBI YOCHANAN BEN MATYA ONCE SAID TO HIS SON: GO OUT AND HIRE WORKERS FOR US. HE WENT AND PROMISED THEM FOOD. BUT WHEN HE CAME TO HIS FATHER, HIS FATHER SAID TO HIM: MY SON, EVEN IF YOU MAKE A MEAL FOR THEM LIKE SOLOMON'S FEAST IN HIS TIME, YOU HAVE NOT FULFILLED YOUR OBLIGATION TOWARD THEM, FOR THEY ARE CHILDREN OF ABRAHAM, ISAAC, AND JACOB.**

RATHER, BEFORE THEY BEGIN WORK, GO OUT AND SAY TO
THEM: ON CONDITION THAT YOU HAVE NO CLAIM ON ME
EXCEPT FOR BREAD AND BEANS.

RABBAN SIMEON BEN GAMALIEL SAYS: RABBI YOCHANAN
BEN MATYA DID NOT NEED TO SAY THIS, FOR EVERYTHING IS
IN ACCORDANCE WITH LOCAL CUSTOM.

Bava Metzia 87a

Gemara: **Rav Acha the son of Rav Joseph said to Rav Chisda:
Did we learn bread made of beans or did we learn BREAD
AND BEANS? Rav Chisda responded: The *vav,* meaning AND,
should be prominent like the rudder of a ship.**

**When Rabbi Simeon ben Gamaliel said that EVERYTHING IS
IN ACCORDANCE WITH LOCAL CUSTOM, what was the
significance of the word EVERYTHING?**

**Its significance was to teach what we have learned in a
baraita: IF SOMEONE HIRED A WORKER AND SAID TO HIM: I WILL PAY
YOU LIKE THE WAGES OF ONE OR TWO OF THE TOWNSPEOPLE, HE MAY
PAY HIM AT THE LOWEST WAGE. THESE ARE THE WORDS OF RABBI
JOSHUA. BUT THE SAGES SAY THAT WE MUST PAY AT THE AVERAGE
WAGE AMONG THE TOWNSPEOPLE.**

Bava Metzia 92a

Mishnah: **A WORKER MAY EAT A CUCUMBER EVEN IF IT COSTS
AS MUCH AS A *DINAR,* OR A DATE EVEN IF IT COSTS AS MUCH
AS A *DINAR.* RABBI ELEAZAR CHISMA SAYS: A WORKER MAY
NOT EAT MORE THAN HIS WAGE. BUT THE SAGES PERMIT IT,
BUT THEY TEACH A PERSON NOT TO BE A GLUTTON AND
SHUT THE DOOR IN HIS OWN FACE.**

Gemara: **Surely the Sages and the first *Tanna* are of the same
opinion. There is a difference between the two opinions.
The difference is BUT THEY TEACH A PERSON NOT TO BE A
GLUTTON. The first *Tanna* does not say anything about
gluttony, whereas the Sages maintain that we should teach
the worker not to be a glutton.**

If you wish, you can say that the difference between them is their opinion regarding the following statement of Rav Assi: Even if he was hired to pick only one bunch of grapes, he may eat it.

Bava Metzia 92a

If you wish, you can say that the difference between them is their opinion regarding the following statement of Rav: I found a secret scroll in the house of Rabbi Chiyya in which it was written that Issi ben Judah commented on the verse, "When you enter your neighbor's vineyard, you may eat as many grapes as you wish, until you are full," and said: The verse refers not just to workers, but to any person who comes upon a vineyard.

And Rav said: Issi would not allow any vineyard owner to survive.

Rav Ashi said: I reported this teaching to Rav Kahana and suggested to him: Perhaps Issi's statement applies to those who work for their meals, for they work and eat.

Rav Kahana replied to Rav Ashi: Even so, a person wants to choose those whom he will hire to harvest his orchard and not allow anyone to start working and eat from it.

Chapter Five

Prompt Payment

שָׂכִיר יוֹם גּוֹבֶה כָּל הַלַּיְלָה, שָׂכִיר לַיְלָה גּוֹבֶה כָּל הַיּוֹם, שָׂכִיר שָׁעוֹת גּוֹבֶה כָּל הַלַּיְלָה וְכָל הַיּוֹם. שָׂכִיר שַׁבָּת, שָׂכִיר חֹדֶשׁ, שָׂכִיר שָׁנָה, שָׂכִיר שָׁבוּעַ, יָצָא בַּיּוֹם, גּוֹבֶה כָּל הַיּוֹם, יָצָא בַּלַּיְלָה, גּוֹבֶה כָּל הַלַּיְלָה וְכָל הַיּוֹם.

תָּנוּ רַבָּנַן: מִנַּיִן לִשְׂכִיר יוֹם שֶׁגּוֹבֶה כָּל הַלַּיְלָה? תַּלְמוּד לוֹמַר "לֹא תָלִין פְּעֻלַּת שָׂכִיר אִתְּךָ עַד בֹּקֶר".

וּמִנַּיִן לִשְׂכִיר לַיְלָה שֶׁגּוֹבֶה כָּל הַיּוֹם? שֶׁנֶּאֱמַר "בְּיוֹמוֹ תִתֵּן שְׂכָרוֹ".

וְאֵימָא אִיפְּכָא.

שְׂכִירוּת אֵינָה מִשְׁתַּלֶּמֶת אֶלָּא בַּסּוֹף.

תָּנוּ רַבָּנַן: מִמַּשְׁמָע שֶׁנֶּאֱמַר "לֹא תָלִין פְּעֻלַּת שָׂכִיר אִתְּךָ" אֵינִי יוֹדֵעַ שֶׁעַד בֹּקֶר? מַה תַּלְמוּד לוֹמַר "עַד בֹּקֶר"? מְלַמֵּד שֶׁאֵינוֹ עוֹבֵר אֶלָּא עַד בֹּקֶר רִאשׁוֹן בִּלְבַד.

מִכָּאן וְאֵילָךְ מַאי?

אָמַר רַב: עוֹבֵר מִשּׁוּם "בַּל תַּשְׁהֶא".

אָמַר רַב יוֹסֵף מַאי קְרָאָה? "אַל תֹּאמַר לְרֵעֲךָ לֵךְ וָשׁוּב וּמָחָר אֶתֵּן וְיֵשׁ אִתָּךְ".

תָּנוּ רַבָּנָן: הָאוֹמֵר לַחֲבֵירוֹ "צֵא שְׂכוֹר לִי פּוֹעֲלִים", שְׁנֵיהֶן אֵין עוֹבְרִין מִשּׁוּם "בַּל תָּלִין", זֶה לְפִי שֶׁלֹּא שְׂכָרָן, וְזֶה לְפִי שֶׁאֵין פְּעוּלָתוֹ אֶצְלוֹ.

הֵיכִי דָמֵי? אִי דְּאָמַר לְהוּ שְׂכַרְכֶם עָלַי, שְׂכָרוֹ עָלָיו הוּא.

The Torah teaches: "You must pay him his wages on his day before the sun sets" (Deut. 24:15) and "The wages of a hired person shall not remain with you overnight until morning" (Lev. 19:13).

Mishnah: **A DAY WORKER COLLECTS HIS WAGES ANY TIME DURING THE FOLLOWING NIGHT. A NIGHT WORKER COLLECTS ANY TIME DURING THE FOLLOWING DAY. AN HOURLY WORKER COLLECTS ALL NIGHT AND ALL DAY. AS FOR SOMEONE HIRED FOR THE WEEK, FOR THE MONTH, FOR THE YEAR, OR FOR SEVEN YEARS, IF HE LEAVES DURING THE DAY, HE COLLECTS ANY TIME DURING THAT DAY; IF HE LEAVES DURING THE NIGHT, HE COLLECTS ANY TIME THAT NIGHT OR THE FOLLOWING DAY.**

Gemara: **Our Rabbis taught in a *baraita:* FROM WHERE DO WE KNOW THAT A DAY WORKER COLLECTS ANY TIME DURING THE FOLLOWING NIGHT? FROM THE VERSE: "THE WAGES OF A HIRED PERSON SHALL NOT REMAIN WITH YOU OVERNIGHT UNTIL MORNING."**

AND FROM WHERE DO WE KNOW THAT A NIGHT WORKER COLLECTS ANY TIME DURING THE FOLLOWING DAY? FROM THE VERSE: "YOU MUST PAY HIM HIS WAGES ON HIS DAY."

The *baraita* thus teaches, as does the Mishnah, that an employer has twelve hours (the night after a day worker and the day after a night worker) in which to pay his worker.

But, suggests the Gemara: **Say the reverse.** Apply the verse "The wages of a hired person shall not remain with you overnight until morning" to the night worker and the verse "You must pay him his wages on his day" to the day worker. If this were the case, the employer would not have a window of twelve hours after the work was completed to pay his worker. He would have to pay the night worker before the night was over and the day worker before sunset.

The Gemara responds: **Wages are not due until work is completed.** Thus the night worker does not have to be paid until the end of the next day and the day worker until the end of the next night.

What's Your Opinion?

Is the Mishnah/*baraita* interpretation of the Torah's law a reasonable one? Would reversing the application of the verses have been more faithful to the spirit of the Torah's law? How does the law have relevance in our own time?

How promptly ought one to pay:

a telephone bill?

a lawyer's bill?

a doctor's bill?

a plumber?

a handyman?

a tutor?

a baby-sitter?

The Gemara now cites another *baraita:* **Our Rabbis taught: From the words, "The wages of a hired person shall not remain with you *overnight*," isn't it clear that the intention is, "until morning"? Why then are the words "until morning" included? They teach that an employer transgresses the prohibition only on the first morning.** This would mean that if an employer delayed payment for several days, he would still be transgressing this law only once.

The Gemara then asks: **But if that is the case, what is the law after the first morning?** It doesn't seem right that one who delays payment day after day is not guilty of transgressing after the first day.

Rav answered: After that, he violates the rabbinic prohibition, "You shall not delay payment."

Rav Joseph said: What is the biblical foundation for this prohibition? It is, "Do not say to your fellow: 'Go and return, and tomorrow I will pay you,' when you have it with you" (Prov. 3:28).

Rav Joseph, the son of Rav Chiyya, was one of the leading Babylonian *Amoraim* during the first part of the fourth century. For a period of time he directed the academy at Pumbedita. He counted Rava and Abaye among his students.

Having settled the issue that the longer an employer delays payment, the more he is in violation of the law, the Gemara turns to a related matter, citing another *baraita:* **Our Rabbis taught: IF SOMEONE SAYS TO HIS FELLOW: "GO AND HIRE WORKERS FOR ME," NEITHER OF THEM VIOLATES THE PROHIBITION, "THE WAGES OF A HIRED PERSON SHALL NOT REMAIN WITH YOU OVERNIGHT," THIS ONE BECAUSE HE DID NOT HIRE THEM, AND THAT ONE BECAUSE THE WORK IS NOT BEING DONE FOR HIM.**

Under what circumstances would this ruling come into play? If the one who hired the workers said to them, "Your wages are my responsibility," then their wages would be his responsibility. If payment was late, he would be in violation of the law.

Bava Metzia 111a

לָא צְרִיכָא, דַּאֲמַר לְהוּ: שְׂכַרְכֶם עַל בַּעַל הַבַּיִת.

יְהוּדָה בַּר מָרֵימָר אֲמַר לֵיה לְשַׁמָּעֵיה: זִיל אַגֵּיר לִי פּוֹעֲלִים, וְאֵימָא לְהוּ: שְׂכַרְכֶם עַל בַּעַל הַבַּיִת.

מָרֵימָר וּמָר זוּטְרָא אָגְרִי לַהֲדָדֵי.

No. This *baraita* comes into play when the one who hires the workers says to them, "Your wages are the responsibility of the employer." Under these circumstances, neither the hirer nor the employer would be guilty were payment delayed.

Judah bar Maremar said to his agent: "Go and hire workers for me and say to them: 'Your wages are the responsibility of the employer.'"

Maremar and Mar Zutra would hire workers for each other.

Even though the Gemara provides biblical foundation for the laws requiring prompt payment of workers, it still includes the *baraita* that shows how employers can hire workers without fear of breaking the law. The Gemara even gives examples of three Sages who made use of this *baraita* in their hiring practices.

Maremar and Mar Zutra, colleagues of Rav Ashi, were Babylonian *Amoraim* at the end of the fourth century and the beginning of the fifth century. Maremar's son, Judah, lived in the fifth century during the last generation of *Amoraim*.

41

What's Your Opinion?

Why was this *baraita* composed? In view of the Gemara's
support for prompt payment of workers, why was this *baraita*
included in the talmudic text? Is there any way to justify the
behavior of Judah bar Maremar, Maremar, and Mar Zutra? Is it
surprising that the Gemara does not disparage their activities?

Bava Metzia 111a

"שְׂכִיר שָׁעוֹת גּוֹבֶה כָּל הַלַּיְלָה וְכָל הַיּוֹם". אָמַר רַב: שְׂכִיר
שָׁעוֹת דְּיוֹם גּוֹבֶה כָּל הַיּוֹם, שְׂכִיר שָׁעוֹת דְּלַיְלָה גּוֹבֶה כָּל
הַלַּיְלָה. וּשְׁמוּאֵל אָמַר: שְׂכִיר שָׁעוֹת דְּיוֹם גּוֹבֶה כָּל הַיּוֹם,
וּשְׂכִיר שָׁעוֹת דְּלַיְלָה גּוֹבֶה כָּל הַלַּיְלָה וְכָל הַיּוֹם.

תְּנַן: שְׂכִיר שָׁעוֹת גּוֹבֶה כָּל הַלַּיְלָה וְכָל הַיּוֹם. תְּיוּבְתָּא דְּרַב.

אָמַר לָךְ רַב: לִצְדָדִין קָתָנֵי: שְׂכִיר שָׁעוֹת דְּיוֹם גּוֹבֶה כָּל
הַיּוֹם, שְׂכִיר שָׁעוֹת דְּלַיְלָה גּוֹבֶה כָּל הַלַּיְלָה.

תְּנַן: הָיָה שְׂכִיר שַׁבָּת, שְׂכִיר חֹדֶשׁ, שְׂכִיר שָׁנָה, שְׂכִיר
שָׁבוּעַ, יוֹצֵא בַּיּוֹם, גּוֹבֶה כָּל הַיּוֹם, יוֹצֵא בַּלַּיְלָה, גּוֹבֶה כָּל
הַלַּיְלָה וְכָל הַיּוֹם.

אָמַר לָךְ רַב: תַּנָּאֵי הִיא; דְּתַנְיָא: שְׂכִיר שָׁעוֹת דְּיוֹם גּוֹבֶה
כָּל הַיּוֹם, שְׂכִיר שָׁעוֹת דְּלַיְלָה גּוֹבֶה כָּל הַלַּיְלָה. דִּבְרֵי רַבִּי
יְהוּדָה. רַבִּי שִׁמְעוֹן אוֹמֵר: שְׂכִיר שָׁעוֹת דְּיוֹם גּוֹבֶה כָּל הַיּוֹם,
שְׂכִיר שָׁעוֹת דְּלַיְלָה גּוֹבֶה כָּל הַלַּיְלָה וְכָל הַיּוֹם.

The Gemara now records a dispute between two *Amoraim*
regarding the Mishnah: **AN HOURLY WORKER COLLECTS ALL
NIGHT AND ALL DAY. Rav said: An hourly worker hired for
the day collects any time that day. An hourly worker hired
for the night collects any time that night. But Samuel said:
An hourly worker hired for the day collects any time that
day. An hourly worker hired for the night collects any time
that night or the following day.**

The Gemara raises an objection to Rav's viewpoint: **We have learned in the Mishnah: AN HOURLY WORKER COLLECTS ALL NIGHT AND ALL DAY. This is a refutation of Rav.**

The Gemara responds: **Rav can say to you: The Mishnah referred to the alternate possibilities. An hourly worker hired for the day collects any time that day. An hourly worker hired for the night collects any time that night.**

The Gemara raises another objection to Rav's position, again citing the Mishnah. **We have learned in the Mishnah: SOMEONE HIRED FOR THE WEEK, FOR THE MONTH, FOR THE YEAR, OR FOR SEVEN YEARS, IF HE LEFT DURING THE DAY, HE COLLECTS ANY TIME DURING THAT DAY; IF HE LEFT DURING THE NIGHT, HE COLLECTS ANY TIME THAT NIGHT AND THE FOLLOWING DAY.** This suggests that when someone completes his work during the night, the employer has through the next day to pay him. This contradicts Rav, who said that he must be paid that night.

The Gemara replies: **Rav can say to you: This is a dispute between *Tannaim*, for it has been taught in a *baraita:* AN HOURLY WORKER HIRED FOR THE DAY COLLECTS ANY TIME THAT DAY. AN HOURLY WORKER HIRED FOR THE NIGHT COLLECTS ANY TIME THAT NIGHT. THESE ARE THE WORDS OF RABBI JUDAH. RABBI SIMEON SAYS: AN HOURLY WORKER HIRED FOR THE DAY COLLECTS ANY TIME THAT DAY. AN HOURLY WORKER HIRED FOR THE NIGHT COLLECTS ANY TIME THAT NIGHT OR THE FOLLOWING DAY.**

This *baraita* gives evidence of two opinions on this matter in tannaitic times. Rabbi Simeon's viewpoint, which gives the employer all the next day to pay the hourly night worker, is reflected in the Mishnah and is supported by Samuel. Rabbi Judah's position, that the hourly night worker must be paid that night, provides foundation for Rav's viewpoint.

When the Mishnah speaks of Rabbi Judah, without his father's name, it refers to Rabbi Judah bar Ilai, who lived during the middle of the second century. He was a student of Rabbi Akiva and was among those who had to be ordained secretly because of persecution by Roman authorities. When the persecution died down, Rabbi Judah took the lead in reconvening the Sanhedrin. He was one of the most learned and respected Rabbis of his time and was recognized as the chief spokesman among the Sages. His opinions are recorded in the Mishnah over 600 times.

Rabbi Simeon bar Yochai, normally called Rabbi Simeon in the Mishnah, was one of the leading students of Rabbi Akiva. His views are often cited as being at odds with those of Rabbi Akiva's other students. Rabbi Simeon spent many years in hiding from the Romans, and an aura of mystery grew up about his life. Numerous stories were told about him as a miracle worker, and until recent times, it was believed by many that he was the author of the *Zohar*. His views are recorded in the Mishnah over 300 times.

The Gemara normally resolves contradictions by applying differing views to different situations. From time to time, however, rather than resolve a contradiction, the Gemara explains it as reflecting a difference of opinion among the *Tannaim*. Such is the case here, where the controversy between the *Amoraim* Rav and Samuel is explained as a reflection of a dispute between the *Tannaim* Rabbi Judah and Rabbi Simeon.

What's Your Opinion?

Which position is more reasonable, Rav's or Samuel's? Which more accurately reflects the intention of the biblical law? Should the employer of an hourly night worker be given the next day to pay him his wages?

Consider This Case

Isaac buys the supplies for his auto business from Federal Wholesalers. Federal allows him thirty days to pay his bills. A representative of Budget Wholesalers approaches Isaac, offering to supply with him the same goods at the same prices as Federal and allow him ninety days to make his payments. Would it be right for Isaac to change from Federal to Budget?

Bava Metzia 111a

אֶחָד שְׂכַר אָדָם וְאֶחָד שְׂכַר בְּהֵמָה וְאֶחָד שְׂכַר כֵּלִים. יֵשׁ בּוֹ
מִשּׁוּם "בְּיוֹמוֹ תִתֵּן שְׂכָרוֹ" וְיֵשׁ בּוֹ מִשּׁוּם "לֹא תָלִין פְּעֻלַּת
שָׂכִיר אִתְּךָ עַד בֹּקֶר". אֵימָתַי? בִּזְמַן שֶׁתְּבָעוֹ, לֹא תְּבָעוֹ, אֵינוֹ
עוֹבֵר עָלָיו.

Mishnah: **THE TORAH'S LAWS, "YOU MUST PAY HIM HIS WAGES ON HIS DAY," AND, "THE WAGES OF A HIRED PERSON SHALL NOT REMAIN WITH YOU OVERNIGHT UNTIL MORNING," APPLY TO HIRING A HUMAN BEING, HIRING AN ANIMAL, AND HIRING UTENSILS.**

WHEN IS THE EMPLOYER DEEMED GUILTY OF VIOLATING THESE LAWS? WHEN THE WORKER CLAIMS HIS PAY. BUT IF HE DOES NOT CLAIM HIS WAGES, THE EMPLOYER IS NOT IN VIOLATION OF THESE LAWS.

What's Your Opinion?

Is it right that an employer who pays late is not considered guilty of violating the law if his employee does not claim his wages at the proper time? Shouldn't the employer be responsible to pay on time regardless of whether or not the worker asks for his wages? How can such a law be justified?

Consider This Case

Richard, a custodian at the University of Washington, was confused about the payments due him. He neglected to claim the check for his work during the first two weeks of March. He was short of funds, struggling to make ends meet, but was unaware that he was missing one paycheck. The check remained in a secretary's desk for two and one-half months. Not until the beginning of June was it discovered that Richard had failed to come to the office to pick up his check.

It is clear that Richard's distress was a result of his own carelessness, but should the university be considered blameless? Should an employer be excused from paying a worker promptly if the worker fails to claim his pay? Should the university be required to compensate Richard for the late payment? Should the university establish a different system for paying its employees?

Bava Metzia 110b-111a

Mishnah: **A DAY WORKER COLLECTS HIS WAGES ANY TIME DURING THE FOLLOWING NIGHT. A NIGHT WORKER COLLECTS ANY TIME DURING THE FOLLOWING DAY. AN HOURLY WORKER COLLECTS ALL NIGHT AND ALL DAY. AS FOR SOMEONE HIRED FOR THE WEEK, FOR THE MONTH, FOR THE YEAR, OR FOR SEVEN YEARS, IF HE LEAVES DURING THE DAY, HE COLLECTS ANY TIME DURING THAT DAY; IF HE LEAVES DURING THE NIGHT, HE COLLECTS ANY TIME THAT NIGHT OR THE FOLLOWING DAY.**

Gemara: **Our Rabbis taught in a *baraita:* FROM WHERE DO WE KNOW THAT A DAY WORKER COLLECTS ANY TIME DURING THE FOLLOWING NIGHT? FROM THE VERSE: "THE WAGES OF A HIRED PERSON SHALL NOT REMAIN WITH YOU OVERNIGHT UNTIL MORNING."**

AND FROM WHERE DO WE KNOW THAT A NIGHT WORKER COLLECTS ANY TIME DURING THE FOLLOWING DAY? FROM THE VERSE: "YOU MUST PAY HIM HIS WAGES ON HIS DAY."

Say the reverse.

Wages are not due until work is completed.

Our Rabbis taught: FROM THE WORDS, "THE WAGES OF A HIRED PERSON SHALL NOT REMAIN WITH YOU *OVERNIGHT,"* ISN'T IT CLEAR THAT THE INTENTION IS, "UNTIL MORNING"? WHY THEN ARE THE WORDS "UNTIL MORNING" INCLUDED? THEY TEACH THAT AN EMPLOYER TRANSGRESSES THE PROHIBITION ONLY ON THE FIRST MORNING.

But if that is the case, what is the law after the first morning?

Rav answered: After that, he violates the rabbinic prohibition, "You shall not delay payment."

Rav Joseph said: What is the biblical foundation for this prohibition? It is, "Do not say to your fellow: 'Go and return, and tomorrow I will pay you,' when you have it with you."

Our Rabbis taught: IF SOMEONE SAYS TO HIS FELLOW: "GO AND HIRE WORKERS FOR ME," NEITHER OF THEM VIOLATES THE PROHIBITION, "THE WAGES OF A HIRED PERSON SHALL NOT REMAIN WITH YOU OVERNIGHT," THIS ONE BECAUSE HE DID NOT HIRE THEM, AND THAT ONE BECAUSE THE WORK IS NOT BEING DONE FOR HIM.

Under what circumstances would this ruling come into play? If the one who hired the workers said to them, "Your wages are my responsibility," then their wages would be his responsibility, and if payment was late, he would be in violation of the law.

Bava Metzia 111a

No. This *baraita* comes into play when the one who hires the workers says to them, "Your wages are the responsibility of the employer." Under these circumstances, neither the hirer nor the employer would be guilty were payment delayed.

Judah bar Maremar said to his agent: "Go and hire workers for me and say to them: 'Your wages are the responsibility of the employer.'"

Maremar and Mar Zutra would hire workers for each other.

Bava Metzia 111a

AN HOURLY WORKER COLLECTS ALL NIGHT AND ALL DAY. Rav said: An hourly worker hired for the day collects any time that day. An hourly worker hired for the night collects any time that night. But Samuel said: An hourly worker hired for the day collects any time that day. An hourly worker hired for the night collects any time that night or the following day.

We have learned in the Mishnah: AN HOURLY WORKER COLLECTS ALL NIGHT AND ALL DAY. This is a refutation of Rav.

Rav can say to you: The Mishnah referred to the alternate possibilities. An hourly worker hired for the day collects any time that day. An hourly worker hired for the night collects any time that night.

We have learned in the Mishnah: SOMEONE HIRED FOR THE WEEK, FOR THE MONTH, FOR THE YEAR, OR FOR SEVEN YEARS, IF HE LEFT DURING THE DAY, HE COLLECTS ANY TIME DURING THAT DAY; IF HE LEFT DURING THE NIGHT, HE COLLECTS ANY TIME THAT NIGHT AND THE FOLLOWING DAY.

Rav can say to you: This is a dispute between *Tannaim,* for it has been taught in a *baraita:* AN HOURLY WORKER HIRED FOR THE DAY COLLECTS ANY TIME THAT DAY. AN HOURLY WORKER HIRED FOR THE NIGHT COLLECTS ANY TIME THAT NIGHT. THESE ARE THE WORDS OF RABBI JUDAH. RABBI SIMEON SAYS: AN HOURLY WORKER HIRED FOR THE DAY COLLECTS ANY TIME THAT DAY. AN HOURLY WORKER HIRED FOR THE NIGHT COLLECTS ANY TIME THAT NIGHT OR THE FOLLOWING DAY.

Bava Metzia 111a

Mishnah: **THE TORAH'S LAWS, "YOU MUST PAY HIM HIS WAGES ON HIS DAY," AND, "THE WAGES OF A HIRED PERSON SHALL NOT REMAIN WITH YOU OVERNIGHT UNTIL MORNING," APPLY TO HIRING A HUMAN BEING, HIRING AN ANIMAL, AND HIRING UTENSILS.**

WHEN IS THE EMPLOYER DEEMED GUILTY OF VIOLATING THESE LAWS? WHEN THE WORKER CLAIMS HIS PAY. BUT IF HE DOES NOT CLAIM HIS WAGES, THE EMPLOYER IS NOT IN VIOLATION OF THESE LAWS.

Chapter Six

Conflicting Claims

Bava Metzia 111a

שָׂכִיר בִּזְמַנּוֹ, נִשְׁבָּע וְנוֹטֵל. עָבַר זְמַנּוֹ, אֵינוֹ נִשְׁבָּע וְנוֹטֵל.

Mishnah: **DURING THE TIME THAT A HIRED PERSON IS TO BE PAID, HE MAY SWEAR THAT HE HAS NOT BEEN PAID AND MAY TAKE HIS WAGES. AFTER THAT TIME PERIOD HAS PASSED, HE MAY NO LONGER SWEAR AND TAKE.**

Bava Metzia 112b

שְׁבוּעָה דְּבַעַל הַבַּיִת הִיא וַעֲקָרוּהָ רַבָּנָן לִשְׁבוּעָה דְּבַעַל הַבַּיִת וְשַׁדְיוּהָ אַשָּׂכִיר, מִשּׁוּם כְּדֵי חַיָּיו דְּשָׂכִיר.

וּמִשּׁוּם כְּדֵי חַיָּיו דְּשָׂכִיר מַפְסַדְנָא לֵיהּ לְבַעַל הַבַּיִת?

בַּעַל הַבַּיִת גּוּפֵיהּ נִיחָא לֵיהּ דְּמִשְׁתַּבַּע שָׂכִיר וְשָׁקֵיל, כִּי הֵיכִי דְּלִיתַּגְּרוּ לֵיהּ פּוֹעֲלִים.

שָׂכִיר גּוּפֵיהּ נִיחָא לֵיהּ דְּמִשְׁתַּבַּע בַּעַל הַבַּיִת וְיִפְקַע, כִּי הֵיכִי דְּלִיגְרוּהוּ.

בַּעַל הַבַּיִת עַל כָּרְחֵיהּ אֲגַר.

שָׂכִיר נַמִי בְּעַל כָּרְחֵיהּ אִתַּגַּר.

Whenever possible, the courts tried to avoid oaths. People didn't want to take even truthful oaths for fear of inadvertently making a mistake and thus swear falsely by God's name. The courts preferred to arrive at the truth through written evidence or through the testimony of witnesses. But in certain instances, conflicting claims could be settled only by having one party or the other take an oath. (The court would never have both opposing claimants take oaths, as this would surely mean that one or the other was swearing falsely.) The question was which party was entitled to swear and have its claim upheld.

אֶלָּא, בַּעַל הַבַּיִת טָרוּד בְּפוֹעֲלִים הוּא.

אִי הָכִי, נֵיתַב לֵיהּ בְּלָא שְׁבוּעָה.

כְּדֵי לְהָפִיס דַּעְתּוֹ שֶׁל בַּעַל הַבַּיִת.

וְנֵיתַב לֵיהּ בְּעֵדִים.
טְרִיחָא לְהוּ מִילְתָא.
וְנֵיתַב לֵיהּ מֵעִיקָּרָא.
שְׁנֵיהֶם רוֹצִים בְּהַקָּפָה.

According to biblical law, it is the defendant, the one from whom money is being claimed, who is allowed to take an oath that he does not owe any money and be exempt of liability. The Gemara explains why, in the case of a worker who claims wages from his employer, the Mishnah rules that it is the worker who may take the oath and then get paid. The Gemara teaches: **The oath should be taken by the employer, but the Rabbis uprooted the employer's oath and turned it over to the employee for the sake of the employee's livelihood.**

The Gemara's explanation suggests that the Rabbis believed that the worker's needs took precedence over those of the employer. The Gemara now begins to question this premise: **And because of the livelihood of the worker, shall we cause a loss to the employer?**

The Gemara replies: **The employer himself is satisfied that the worker swears and takes his wages in order that workers will hire themselves out to him.** No employer wants to be known as one who withholds payment of workers' wages.

But, says the Gemara, the opposite can be said: **The worker himself is satisfied that the employer swear and be exempt in order that the employer will hire him.** A worker who is suspected of claiming wages not due him is unlikely to be hired.

The Gemara rejects this argument: **The employer is forced to hire workers.** His need for workers will outweigh any hesitation he may have about hiring.

Again the Gemara makes the opposite argument: **The worker also is forced to hire himself out.** Because he must have work, he won't be especially concerned about the reputation of the employer.

Since each reason for allowing the worker to swear and take his wages is turned around and applied to the employer, the Gemara offers another reason why the Rabbis gave the oath to the worker: **Rather, the employer is busy dealing with many workers.** Since the employer has to pay many workers, while the worker has only one employer to deal with, it is less likely that the worker will make a mistake as to whether or not he was paid. This is the reason the Rabbis gave the oath to the worker.

The Gemara responds: **If so, let the employer pay him without requiring an oath of him.** Let the employer believe a worker who says that he has not been paid and not require an oath of him.

The Gemara explains: **It is in order to set the mind of the employer at ease.** If the employer thinks that he may have already paid the worker his wages, the fact that the worker takes an oath assures him that he hasn't.

What's Your Opinion?

In a situation where a worker claims his wages and the employer says that he has already paid him, is it right that the worker be allowed to swear that he wasn't paid and then receive the payment? Do you believe that this practice can be justified because the worker's need for his livelihood takes precedence over the employer's need for profit? Do you believe that this practice can be justified because the employer has many workers and many payments to keep in mind, whereas the worker has only one employer and one payment to remember?

The Gemara now makes another suggestion altogether. Instead of making a change in who takes the oath: **Let the employer pay the worker in the presence of witnesses.** Then witnesses would be able to testify as to whether or not the employee was paid.

The Gemara responds: **That would be a lot of trouble for them** to have to assemble witnesses every time a worker was to be paid.

The Gemara then submits another proposal: **Let the employer pay the worker in advance.** If it were mandated that the worker be paid before he begins working, then there would be no questions later about whether or not he was paid.

But this proposal is also rejected: **Both the employer and the worker prefer that the worker receive a credit for his labor.** The employer may not want to pay before he has seen that the work was performed to his satisfaction. The worker may not want to be paid in advance because he may not have a safe place to keep his money while he is working.

What's Your Opinion?

The Gemara suggests two ways to avoid disputes about whether or not a worker was paid. One is to have witnesses observe when wages are paid. The other is to always pay workers in advance. Both suggestions are rejected in the Gemara. Can you think of other measures that might have been suggested to avoid such disputes?

Bava Metzia 112b-113a

אִי הָכִי, אֲפִילוּ עָבַר זְמַנּוֹ נַמִי. אַלָּמָה תְּנַן: עָבַר זְמַנּוֹ אֵינוֹ נִשְׁבָּע וְנוֹטֵל?

חֲזָקָה אֵין בַּעַל הַבַּיִת עוֹבֵר מִשּׁוּם "בַּל תָּלִין".

וְהָא אָמְרַתְּ בַּעַל הַבַּיִת טָרוּד בְּפוֹעֲלָיו הוּא.

הָנֵי מִילֵי מִקַּמֵּיה דְּלִימְטְיֵיה זְמַן חִיּוּבֵיה, אֲבָל מְטָא זְמַן חִיּוּבֵיה, רָמֵי אַנַּפְשֵׁיה וּמִידְכַּר.

וְכִי שָׂכִיר עוֹבֵר מִשּׁוּם "בַּל תִּגְזֹל"?

הָתָם תְּרֵי חֲזָקֵי, הָכָא חֲדָא חֲזָקָה. גַּבֵּי בַּעַל הַבַּיִת אִיכָּא תְּרֵי חֲזָקֵי: חֲדָא דְּאֵין בַּעַל הַבַּיִת עוֹבֵר מִשּׁוּם "בַּל תָּלִין", וַחֲדָא דְּאֵין שָׂכִיר מַשְׁהֵא שְׂכָרוֹ. וְהָכָא, חֲדָא חֲזָקָה.

If, when there is a dispute about whether or not the worker has been paid, it is assumed that it is the employer who is in error, then, says the Gemara: **Even if the time period in which the worker should be paid has passed, he should still be allowed to swear and get paid. Why did the Mishnah teach: AFTER THAT TIME PERIOD HAS PASSED, HE MAY NO LONGER SWEAR AND TAKE?**

The Gemara answers: **The presumption is that the employer does not transgress the law, "The wages of a hired person shall not remain with you overnight until morning."**

The Gemara raises an objection to this answer: **But you said that the employer is busy with many workers.** And if so, how can it be presumed that he will not forget to pay his workers on time?

The Gemara replies: **It is only during the time that the workers are to be paid that the employer is busy. Once the period has passed, he takes special pains to remember whom he has paid.**

The Gemara has made the assumption that the employer would not violate the law, "The wages of a hired person shall not remain with you overnight until morning." Now the Gemara asks: **And would the worker break the law, "You shall not rob"?** If it is assumed that the employer would not break the law to pay on time, then the worker who is claiming that he was not paid must be a robber, trying to get double payment. Why should it be assumed that the worker would break the law?

The Gemara replies: **There are two presumptions as opposed to one presumption. There are two presumptions which favor the employer, that an employer does not transgress the law, "The wages of a hired person shall not remain with you overnight until morning," and that a worker does not delay in claiming his wages. While there is only one presumption favoring the worker,** that he would not violate the law against robbery. Thus, after the time period in which the worker is to be paid, the Gemara holds that there is a stronger case to believe the employer than the worker.

What's Your Opinion?

The law, then, is that during the payment period, the worker has the advantage, for if there is a dispute, he may swear and take his wages.

But after the payment period, the employer is given the advantage. In case of a dispute then, the employer may swear that he already paid and is exempt of liability.

Do you believe that this is a good and just law? Do you believe that the Mishnah and the Gemara lean too much one way or the other in favoring the worker or the employer? Explain your viewpoint.

Consider This Case

George, the sales manager at Town Center TV, announced to his salespeople that if, as a group, they exceeded $5 million in sales during the month of December, he would give each of them a Palm Pilot as a gift. They sold more than $6 million in electronic equipment that month, and George was happy to make good on his promise.

The sales staff was made up of seventeen persons; George ordered seventeen Palm Pilots and kept them in his office. The salespeople were invited to come into George's office to receive their gift and to receive the personal congratulations of their boss. He asked them to come within the next day or two. When Herbert came to George's office a week later to pick up his gift, George said that he was certain that he had already given Herbert his Palm Pilot. In fact, all of the Palm Pilots had been distributed.

Herbert said that he had not come previously and that George was mistaken.

What should be done?

Bava Metzia 111a

Mishnah: **DURING THE TIME THAT A HIRED PERSON IS TO BE PAID, HE MAY SWEAR THAT HE HAS NOT BEEN PAID AND MAY TAKE HIS WAGES. AFTER THAT TIME PERIOD HAS PASSED, HE MAY NO LONGER SWEAR AND TAKE.**

Bava Metzia 112b

Gemara: **The oath should be taken by the employer, but the Rabbis uprooted the employer's oath and turned it over to the employee for the sake of the employee's livelihood.**

And because of the livelihood of the worker, shall we cause a loss to the employer?

The employer himself is satisfied that the worker swears and takes his wages in order that workers will hire themselves out to him.

The worker himself is satisfied that the employer swear and be exempt in order that the employer will hire him.

The employer is forced to hire workers.

The worker also is forced to hire himself out.

Rather, the employer is busy dealing with many workers.

If so, let the employer pay him without requiring an oath of him.

It is in order to set the mind of the employer at ease.

Let the employer pay the worker in the presence of witnesses.

That would be a lot of trouble for them.

Let the employer pay the worker in advance.

Both the employer and the worker prefer that the worker receive a credit for his labor.

Bava Metzia 112b-113a

Even if the time period in which the worker should be paid has passed, he should still be allowed to swear and get paid. Why did the Mishnah teach: AFTER THAT TIME PERIOD HAS PASSED, HE MAY NO LONGER SWEAR AND TAKE?

The presumption is that the employer does not transgress the law, "The wages of a hired person shall not remain with you overnight until morning."

But you said that the employer is busy with many workers.

It is only during the time that the workers are to be paid that the employer is busy. Once the period has passed, he takes special pains to remember whom he has paid.

And would the worker break the law, "You shall not rob"?

There are two presumptions as opposed to one presumption. There are two presumptions which favor the employer, that an employer does not transgress the law, "The wages of a hired person shall not remain with you overnight until morning," and that a worker does not delay in claiming his wages. While there is only one presumption favoring the worker.

Chapter Seven

Wrapping It Up

The Employment Contract

How does the Talmud answer each of the following questions?

1. If a worker is hired to do a job and, the day before he is to begin working, he is informed that his services are not needed, what recourse docs he have?

2. If a worker goes to a place of work and then learns that he is not needed, does the employer have to pay him?

3. If a worker refuses to do a job that he promised to do and the job is one that cannot be delayed, what can the employer do?

4. If a worker refuses to do a job that he promised to do and other workers are available, what recourse does the employer have?

Half a Job

Complete the following sentences.

1. If a worker quits after doing half a job and the cost of wages rises, the Rabbis ruled that _____.

2. If a worker quits after doing half a job and the cost of wages rises, Rabbi Dosa ruled that _____.

The Workday

True or false?

1. When it comes to determining the length of the workday, local custom is the determining factor.

2. Since Resh Lakish's ruling is based on a biblical verse, it supersedes local custom.

Eating on the Job

Fill in the blank.

1. Someone who works with produce that is _____ may eat while working as long as the work is being finished.

2. A worker _____ if the produce does not grow from the earth.

3. If someone was _____ on one kind of fruit, he may not eat of another kind of fruit.

4. In determining that a worker's pay should be determined by local custom, the Rabbis meant that the worker should be paid _____.

5. Even though there were no restrictions on the amount that a worker was allowed to eat, the Rabbis taught that a person should not be a _____.

Prompt Payment

Explain the following.

1. Why did the law require prompt payment of workers?

2. Why is an employer given all the next night to pay a day worker for his labor?

3. Why did Maremar and Mar Zutra hire workers for each other?

4. Why is an employer not guilty of paying late if the worker fails to claim his pay?

When a Worker Claims that He Was Not Paid

Which is the correct answer?

1. A worker who claims that he was not paid:

   a) May claim his pay and receive his wages.

   b) May swear that he was not paid and receive his wages.

   c) May bear resentment against an employer who says that he was already paid, but the court will not force the employer to pay him.

2. An oath is required of the worker:

   a) In order to reassure the employer that the claim for wages is honest.

   b) Because it is assumed, without an oath, that the worker's claim is false.

   c) Because all claims had to be supported by oaths.

3. Workers are not, as a rule, paid in front of witnesses:

   a) Because witnesses cannot be trusted.

   b) Because the workers would object.

   c) Because it is too much trouble to assemble witnesses each time workers are paid.

Whom Does the Law Favor?

The law protects workers in the following ways:

1. A worker who comes to a job and finds that there is no work to do must be compensated by the employer.

2. If a worker reneges on a contract to do a job, and the employer is able to find a replacement at no extra charge, the employer has grounds for resentment against the worker for making him go to the trouble of finding a replacement but will not be granted any monetary compensation.

3. An employer may not impose working conditions on a worker that are contrary to local custom.

4. A worker who is harvesting produce may eat as much of that produce as he wishes while he is on the job.

5. Workers must be paid promptly after completing their work.

6. If a dispute arises as to whether or not a worker has received payment for his labor, the worker may take an oath and receive his wages.

The law protects employers in the following ways:

1. If a worker comes to do a job and finds that there is no work to do, if the employer had checked the field the night before and at that time there was work to do, then the employer does not have to compensate the worker.

2. If a worker reneges on a contract to do a job that cannot be delayed, the employer may deceive the worker or may charge him for the cost of replacing him.

3. An employee may not claim benefits or working conditions that are contrary to local custom.

4. If a worker fails to claim his pay, his employer is not required to pay him on time.

5. If a dispute arises as to whether or not a worker has received payment for his labor, and the worker fails to claim his pay on time, then he may not receive his wages without bringing proof to support his claim.

As a general statement, can it be said that the law of the Talmud:

1. Favors the worker?

2. Favors the employer?

3. Seeks justice and does not favor one side or the other?

In what ways can the laws of the Talmud be applied to employer-employee relationships today?

In what ways, if any, will your thinking or behavior be affected as a result of having studied the laws of the Talmud governing employer-employee relationships?

Sources for Further Study

The standard Talmud has had the same pagination since the 1520s, when the first printed edition of the complete Talmud was published in Venice. Each sheet is numbered, front and back, as "a" and "b." In *Talmud for Everyday Living*, it is indicated where each selection can be found in the standard Talmud. Thus, for example, the first selection in our book comes from *Bava Metzia* 75b, which is from the back side of page 75 in the tractate *Bava Metzia*. This information is important for those who are seeking further information about the passages under discussion.

There are two excellent English-language commentaries on *Bava Metzia*. One is *The Talmud: The Steinsaltz Edition*, commentary by Adin Steinsaltz and published in New York by Random House. The six volumes on *Bava Metzia* appeared between 1989 and 1993. The passage from *Bava Metzia* 75b can be found at the beginning of volume 5. *The Steinsaltz Edition* contains two translations of the Hebrew/Aramaic text; one is a literal translation, and the other is an annotated translation with a running commentary. Additional notes are added when deemed necessary, as well as brief biographies of the principal Sages, and comments on places, customs, and language usage, all of which help clarify and edify the talmudic text.

The other English commentary on *Bava Metzia* is part of *The Schottenstein Edition,* published in New York by Mesorah Publications in three volumes between 1992 and 1994. It has one translation/commentary with extensive additional notes at the bottom of each page. Page 75b can be found near the end of volume 2. A student who wishes to find a more detailed analysis of the Talmud's passages than that offered in our book would do well to consult either of the above mentioned works.

Persons with an interest in rabbinic literature should have in their library *Introduction to the Talmud and Midrash* by Gunter Stemberger (Edinburgh: T&T Clark, 1996). It gives the reader an overview of scholarly opinion on all aspects of the Talmud and related literature. It has a summary of the content of each tractate of the Mishnah, a small biography of many of the Sages, and a discussion of how the various texts were composed and edited. It also includes extensive bibliographies.

The Literature of the Sages, First Part (Assen/Maastricht, Philadelphia: Van Gorcum, Fortress Press, 1987), edited by Shmuel Safrai, is also a very useful volume for the English reader. Although this work does not contain the variety of scholarly views as found in Stemberger's work, Safrai's book is more readable. The chapters by Abraham Goldberg on the Mishnah, the *Tosefta,* the Palestinian Talmud, and the Babylonian Talmud are to be especially recommended as lucid and highly informative.

For a more traditional view of the Talmud, one may turn to the introductory volume to *The Steinsaltz Edition.* It is called *A Reference Guide* by Adin Steinsaltz (New York: Random House, 1989). It gives historical background, lists of Rabbis, explanations of talmudic terminology, weights and measures, and much more. Students of the Talmud who own this book will find that they turn to it frequently and that it is repeatedly helpful.

For those who wish to pursue the study of employer-employee relations in Jewish law beyond the period of the Talmud, two books by Meir Tamari will be useful. His 1987 work, *With All Your Possessions: Jewish Ethics and Economic Life* (New York: The Free Press, Collier Macmillan Publishers) has a chapter on "Wages and Labor," and his 1995 book, *The Challenge of Wealth* (Northvale, N.J.: Jason Aronson) contains a section called "Ethical Issues in Corporate Labor Policies." Both of these works bring the teachings of the Talmud and later Jewish codes and responsa to bear on modern labor-management matters.

Aaron Levine has written extensively on business issues from a Jewish ethical perspective. His latest book, *Case Studies in Jewish Business Ethics* (Hoboken, N.Y.: Ktav Publishing House, Yeshiva University Press, 2000), contains a chapter on labor relations in which he applies rabbinic rulings throughout the centuries to present-day questions facing employers and workers.

Those who wish to expand their English language study of the Talmud will find guidance from the works of Judith Abrams. Her books, all published by Jason Aronson (Northvale, New Jersey and London) are *Learn Talmud* (1989), *The Talmud for Beginners, Volumes I, II and III* (1993-1997) and *A Beginner's Guide to the Steinsaltz Talmud* (1999). Abrams has selected thoughtful and stimulating Talmudic passages and writes with a passion showing how the uninitiated can learn Talmud using the Steinsaltz Edition.

Clearly, there is no end to the study of the Talmud and Jewish law. One page leads to the next, and one book leads to the next. It is this writer's hope that consulting the works here recommended will not only increase readers' knowledge, but will motivate the reader toward further study.